FIRST ST...
DRESSMAKING

ESSENTIAL STITCHES AND SEAMS
EASY GARMENT MAKING
INDIVIDUALIZING TISSUE-PAPER PATTERNS

British Library Cataloguing-in-Publication Data
A catalogue record for this book is available from the
British Library

Dressmaking and Tailoring

Dressmaking and Tailoring broadly refers to those who make, repair or alter clothing for a profession. A dressmaker will traditionally make custom clothing for women, ranging from dresses and blouses to full evening gowns (also historically called a mantua-maker or a modiste). Whereas a tailor will do the same, but usually for men's clothing - especially suits. The terms essentially refer to a specific set of hand and machine sewing skills, as well as pressing techniques that are unique to the construction of traditional clothing. This is separate to 'made to measure', which uses a set of pre-existing patterns. Usually, a bespoke tailored suit or dress will be completely original and unique to the customer, and hence such items have been highly desirable since the trade first appeared in the thirteenth century. The Oxford English Dictionary states that the word 'tailor' first came into usage around the 1290s, and undoubtedly by this point, tailoring guilds, as well as those of cloth merchants and weavers were well established across Europe.

As the tailoring profession has evolved, so too have the methods of tailoring. There are a number of distinctive business models which modern tailors may practice, such as 'local tailoring' where the tailor is met locally, and the garment is produced locally too, 'distance tailoring', where a garment is ordered from an out-of-town tailor, enabling cheaper labour to be used -

which, in practice can now be done on a global scale via e-commerce websites, and a 'travelling tailor', where the man or woman will travel between cities, usually stationing in a luxury hotel to provide the client the same tailoring services they would provide in their local store. These processes are the same for both women's and men's garment making.

Pattern making is a very important part of this profession; the construction of a paper or cardboard template from which the parts of a garment are traced onto fabric before cutting our and assembling. A custom dressmaker (or tailor) frequently employs one of three pattern creation methods; a 'flat-pattern method' which begins with the creation of a sloper or block (a basic pattern for a garment, made to the wearer's measurements), which can then be used to create patterns for many styles of garments, with varying necklines, sleeves, dart placements and so on. Although it is also used for womenswear, the 'drafting method' is more commonly employed in menswear and involves drafting a pattern directly onto pattern paper using a variety of straightedges and curves. Since menswear rarely involves draping, pattern-making is the primary preparation for creating a cut-and-sew woven garment. The third method, the 'pattern draping method' is used when the patternmaker's skill is not matched with the difficulty of the design. It involves creating a muslin mock-up pattern, by pinning fabric directly on a dress form, then transferring the muslin outline and markings onto a paper pattern or using the muslin as the pattern itself.

Dressmaking and tailoring has become a very well respected profession; dressmakers such as Pierre Balmain, Christian Dior, Cristóbal Balenciaga and Coco Chanel have gone on to achieve international acclaim and fashion notoriety. Balmain, known for sophistication and elegance, once said that 'dressmaking is the architecture of movement.' Whilst tailors, due to the nature of their profession - catering to men's fashions, have not garnered such levels of individual fame, areas such as 'Savile Row' in the United Kingdom are today seen as the heart of the trade.

·PREFACE

Probably no subject is of such vital interest to women as clothes.
Always to be suitably and becomingly dressed—this is indeed an
ambition toward which every woman aspires. But what does this
involve? First of all, the ability to select the right colours, fabrics,
and designs for her type and needs. And secondly, if she must dress
on a modest income, the ability to make smart, attractive clothes.

This book lays the foundation for this ability. It takes up the
necessary sewing tools, the making of the stitches and seams that
are used in all garments, the way to apply this information in
making several very attractive garments for which no patterns are
needed, and the use of patterns and their adjustment for perfect
fitting. Equipped with such information, a woman is prepared to
make garments of a simple nature and to undertake a study of the
more interesting processes of cutting, fitting, and finishing dresses.

In a study of *Essential Stitches and Seams*, the important points to
learn are how to handle all the tools that a dressmaker uses, including the sewing machine, and how to make with perfection the
various stitches that are used in sewing. It is indeed true that the
greater one's experience, the better will be one's workmanship.
But a good slogan to adopt from the very start is, " Perfection in the
smallest detail."

To provide examples for immediate practice, several garments
for which almost every woman has need, are included in *Easy Garment Making*. These provide training in cutting material without
patterns, making seams, cutting and piecing bias strips, making
hems and plackets, applying pockets, shoulder straps, bindings,
facings, and many other types of foundation finishes. The complete directions and very clear illustrations given for them will
enable any woman to make garments which she will be proud to wear.

The excellent patterns obtainable to-day make dressmaking a
possibility for every woman. But to achieve smart results, it is
necessary to take one's measurements correctly in order to
determine the correct size, to alter patterns for irregularities
of figure, and to make a guide pattern for checking up other

patterns. All these matters are thoroughly explained and illustrated in the Section, *Individualizing Tissue-Paper Patterns*. With
such knowledge, patterns will serve the true purpose for which
they are intended—accurate cutting guides for modish and correct-
fitting garments.

Throughout this book, illustrations are used to make the sewing
instructions absolutely clear. In fact, so well are the various
articles and sewing processes pictured that the study of the text
becomes a simple and fascinating task.

A woman who masters these first steps of dressmaking has made a
good start in learning how to sew. As she advances, she will acquire
a training that will enable her, besides making her own clothes, to
become a professional dressmaker should she so desire. In entering
this field, which is a large one, she may do general dressmaking or
she may specialize in some phase of it that particularly appeals to
her. Thus she puts herself in a position to enjoy the delights of
independence.

CONTENTS

ESSENTIAL STITCHES AND SEAMS

ESSENTIAL STITCHES AND SEAMS

ACQUIRING SEWING SKILL

1. To wish for lovely clothes, to be particular about their fit and finish, to recognize the importance of the small but significant details of dress is one of the most feminine of dreams, but a dream that is most readily made a reality. First of all, consider the mastery of the essentials of sewing, leading to the perfection of accomplishment that is characteristic of fine dressmaking and high grade tailoring, add to this the natural creative impulse, well-directed, and from the combination obtain the ability to select and develop clothes that are individual, suitable and becoming.

Besides the resulting pleasure, so completely one's own, and to be cherished and fostered by every woman, there is profit too, for she who sews with skill holds in her hands the magic key that opens the door to chic.

2. The study of the art of dress—the construction of clothes, the personality of clothes, the effectiveness of clothes—may be likened to a journey into new lands, where one meets with new experiences and forms new appreciations and realizations. On every hand romance is to be found, rich experiences are to be had, and opportunity for the development of taste and discrimination in dress and of appreciation of beauty, all so essential to the happiness and culture of all women, is to be met.

To know how to use the needle and the sewing machine, to cut out and to sew pieces of cloth together, besides being essential to the development of sewing skill, are extremely interesting ; and to be able to create exquisitely beautiful articles or garments is a most gratifying and worthy accomplishment, proving not only of definite economic value but of cultural value as well. To create a beautiful gown is indeed as much a work of art as to paint a beautiful picture, for it embraces all the skill and all the knowledge of colour and line that the true artist has at his command.   In fact, the doors of achievement stand open to the fashion artist or to any one who makes a specialty of needlecraft.

3. Before you take up the study of dressmaking, you must consider many points that have to do with ultimate success. First of all, you should bear in mind that poor work is absolutely valueless ; there is no place in sewing for carelessness of any kind. Set a high ideal and make an untiring effort to reach it.

Take an active interest in clothes, so that you may obtain a knowledge of what others are wearing—the material, the style, the workmanship—and thus appreciate the good and avoid the bad.

Encourage self-criticism ; do not consider any work as satisfactory unless it is the best that you can possibly do, regardless of whether it is to be seen by others or not. Application, and industry, as well as concentration and effort, are of utmost importance.

Pay close attention to the valuable points brought out in the text and apply them diligently, so that you will become thoroughly familiar with every detail ; and in this connection remember all the while that perseverance, judgment, accuracy, and imagination, as well as skill in construction are absolutely necessary.

Some persons sew for pleasure, some for duty, some for profit ; but whether you sew for any of these things or all of them, the element of time must be considered. To sew successfully does not mean that you must accomplish a certain amount of work within a given time ; your aim, rather, should be to strive for a high standard of excellence and technical skill. Sewing is work that cannot be done well in a haphazard way ; the person who does such work must be careful and painstaking.

Self-confidence is a valuable asset in sewing ; you should ever remember that if you have confidence in yourself others will have confidence in you. Therefore, never take up any lesson in a half-hearted manner ; rather, be determined that you are going to master it, It will always prove ready to help you in becoming proficient and will also create in you a desire for beautiful things. Success will surely come if you study the lessons carefully, apply the instructions faithfully, and think and reason out the problems thoroughly.

MAKING ESSENTIAL STITCHES AND SEAMS

METHOD OF STUDY

4. The purpose of this lesson is to teach you how to make the essential, or foundation, stitches and seams used in sewing ; how to train your hand to use the needle, the scissors, and the thimble ; and how to train your eye to discern the correctness of every stitch, to measure distance, and to keep a precise or even line.

After you learn the principles of the essential stitches, you take up more advanced work, and gradually you acquire sufficient skill and confidence to cut out and make dresses, coats, and other wearing apparel of the more costly materials. You will also be able to make use of the suggestions relating to styles and trimmings that are taken up later and to adapt them to current fashions.

5. Advantages of Making Samplers.—As you take up this lesson, you may feel that you are so familiar with the foundation stitches and seams that you do not need the work here outlined. But no matter how much experience you may have had in this connection, it will be to your advantage to read the instruction matter carefully and to make the samplers and submit those required for inspection. The work to be done will take very little time if you are accustomed to using the needle, and you will be rewarded by the fact that you know just the correct way in which to make each of these foundation stitches and seams. An additional advantage is that you will become familiar with their correct names, and in this way will not be confused when they are mentioned.

If you are not familiar with the essential stitches and seams, you should practice them diligently until you can make all of them perfectly. Follow the text carefully and study each illustration closely, observing just how the needle is placed in each instance and the way in which the material is held. If you take time to make perfect stitches, you will acquire speed and accuracy with continued practice.

6. Value of Tidiness.—It is absolutely necessary that you be tidy, clean, and careful in carrying on your sewing. Have a definitely arranged place, even if it is only one corner of a room, for your sewing basket or work box, your tools, and your accessories, and keep all these things there.

Keep your hands and finger nails clean, and if your fingers are rough from other work, begin at once to get them in as good condition as possible by the use of hand lotions frequently applied. A worth while habit is that of using a small amount of the special preparation that suits you best each time your hands have been in water. In this way, you will avoid the annoyance of having your thread or the material on which you are working roughen up, as so frequently happens when the nails and hands are not as smooth as they should be. When sewing on white or dainty articles, it is a good plan to have talcum powder on hand, as this, dusted on the hands, helps to absorb perspiration and keep the work clean.

SEWING MATERIALS AND TOOLS

7. Certain equipment is necessary for sewing. The amount of this will depend somewhat on the extent of the sewing you intend to do. The essential equipment for a beginner consists of needles, pins, thread, scissors, thimble, and tape measure. A good plan is to provide just these actual necessities at the beginning and then to add to them as time goes on and your needs increase until you have in your possession a selection of sewing aids that will not only save time for you but also help you to do the best work of which you are capable.

The various articles included in the equipment necessary to successful results in sewing of all types may be divided into various groups, such as, *cutting* equipment, *measuring and marking* equipment, *sewing* equipment, *pressing* equipment, and *fitting* equipment. These are discussed in the following articles.

8. Cutting Equipment.—Because the first step in the actual construction of an article or garment is cutting, the equipment necessary for this important process is considered first. In Fig. 1 is shown a group of shears and scissors that make up a complete collection. If but one can be supplied, the *shears*, shown at *a*, which may measure from 7 to 9 inches, are best. Next in order of importance are the *bent trimmers*, shown at *b*, which will be found easy to use when cutting out garments because the handles are so placed as to produce one straight edge. A pair of *small-size scissors*, like those shown at *c*, are needed for clipping threads and fabric. *Pinking shears*, shown at *d*, are a valuable aid in sewing as they finish edges with pinking as you cut them, thus making any other finish unnecessary. *Buttonhole scissors*, shown at *e*, are equipped with a small screw to regulate the length of the slash for the buttonhole.

9. A *table* is very necessary for successful cutting. The ideal size is one long enough to lay out the average dress length of 4 yards and this should be supplied for a dressmaking shop. In a home, however, such a table would be difficult to accommodate and in its place you may use the largest one you can conveniently provide.

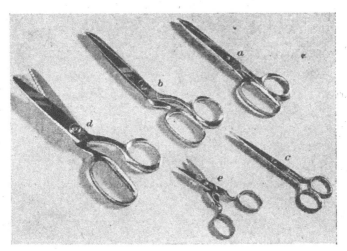

FIG. I

A cutting board of approximately 3 by 4 feet or a section of beaver board this size will be found an acceptable substitute. This can be placed over your dining room table, on a bed, or even on the floor while you are cutting, and then stored away when not in use.

10. Measuring and Marking Equipment.—Necessary aids to accuracy, the importance of which cannot be over estimated, are the various types of measuring and marking accessories, illustrated in Fig. 2. The *tape measure*, *a*, firmly woven and evenly marked, the *yard-stick*, *b*, and the *ruler*, *c*, which may be 15 or 18 inches long, will help you to measure efficiently. The *dressmaker's gauge*, *d*, a handy sewing device accompanying this lesson, has many uses, such as the marking of widths, spaces, scallops, arrowheads, and crowfeet. *Tailor's chalk* in two colours, dark and light, at *e* and *f*, and the *tracing wheel* at *g* are used for marking certain materials. Tailor's chalk can be used on any fabric, but, as a rule, it is employed chiefly for wool. The tracing wheel should be confined to cottons, and only those of the firm type whose threads will not be cut by its sharp points.

11. Sewing Equipment.—When cutting and marking have been completed, you are ready to sew, and to do this properly you will need the equipment shown in Fig. 3.

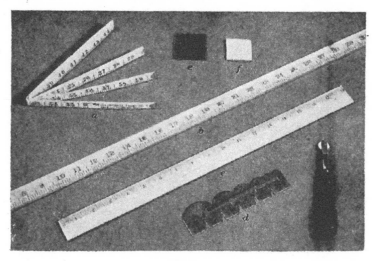

FIG. 2

12. Basting thread, shown at *a*, is made especially for basting purposes. It has a hard, glazed finish, it breaks easily, and does not become embedded in the material. Such thread comes on large spools in only one size and is usually white.

Sewing thread, shown at *b*, is of three kinds, silk, cotton and linen. Sewing silk is intended for use on silks and woollens. Buttonhole twist, a special type of silk thread used in tailoring and for ornamental stitching, is made in black, white and colours, and in various thicknesses. Cotton thread is used on cotton and linen fabrics and comes in white, black and a wide range of colours, and in various sizes, the higher the number the finer the thread. Mercerized cotton, that is, thread having a glossy effect, is available in all colours and is used for cotton, silk, wool and rayon.

13. Pins are a necessity in dressmaking. Used freely in pinning patterns in place and in holding seams together both in basting and fitting, they will be found very helpful. Buy only good pins with fine sharp points, preferably the quality available in boxes, as at *c*. These pins can be procured in various lengths, the medium size being most generally employed. In large establishments, where there is a great deal of sewing done on net, lace, and other open weaves, the longer pins are most satisfactory, while in tailoring, the shortest type is often preferred.

As an aid in using pins, a small **pin cushion,** as at *d*, is a great convenience. Made of a firm wool cloth, with pinked edges, it may be stuffed with horsehair or with tiny clippings of wool cloth.

FIG. 3

14. Needles, a package of which is shown at *e*, range in size from 1 to 12, No. 1 being the coarsest and No. 12 the finest. Needles of average length having round eyes are called *sharps*, while long needles of the same type are known as *milliner's needles*, these two kinds being the ones in most general use.

Needles having long eyes and pointed ends, are called *embroidery*, *crewel*, or *darning* needles, while those with long eyes and blunt ends are known as *tapestry* and *bodkin* or *tape* needles. These have special uses in sewing, as their names imply. Embroidery needles, however, are preferred to regulation needles for ordinary sewing by many persons because of the ease with which the long eyes can be threaded.

It is recommended that a package of assorted sizes, 5 to 10, be provided, also a package all one size, such as 7 or 8. Size 8 is considered about right for use in fine sewing and dressmaking, although size 7 may be preferred by some.

Machine needles are designated as to size by letter or number, depending on the manufacturer, each company making needles to suit its own particular sewing machines. The medium size is recommended for general use.

15. An **emery bag**, shown at *f*, will be found useful in keeping your needles in good condition. Passing a needle back and forth through the emery removes any rust on it and sharpens the point. Do not leave a needle in an emery bag, however, for it seems to collect rust.

16. The **thimble**, shown at *g*, is one of the most helpful aids in hand sewing, it being used to push the needle through the material. Thimbles are made of a variety of materials, such as silver, gold, aluminium, celluloid, and bakelite. They may be of the type shown, or they may be made with an open top, these being preferred by some sewers, especially tailors. The sizes of thimbles range from 6 to 11. In selecting a thimble, have it fit the middle finger snugly when the end of the finger is inserted well into it.

17. Pressing Equipment.—The various articles used in pressing are just as important a part of sewing equipment as any of those used in the actual sewing process, because the finished appearance of an article or garment will not be good unless it receives a pressing after each step of its making and a general pressing when it is completed. Of course, much of the pressing equipment is a part of every household, but if dressmaking is to be done as a profession, an extra set should be provided and kept close to the location at which the sewing is done.

18. Irons, for the ideal arrangement, should be supplied in two sizes, a medium-sized one for general pressing and a small one with a pointed end for fine seams, narrow ruffles, and the like.

19. An **ironing board**, well padded and covered with a clean smooth cloth that can readily be changed, is constantly needed.

Usually a stand accompanies the board, but if not, one of a steady, durable type should be provided.

A **sleeve board**, also well padded and covered, will be found most helpful for the pressing of sleeves and small surfaces.

A **pressing cushion**, consisting of two oval sections, measuring about 12 × 20 inches, of heavy muslin, which have been boiled to remove all dressing, sewed together, and stuffed firmly with clippings of material, will aid you in pressing armhole seams as well as any other curved joinings.

20. **Press cloths** are necessities and should be especially provided for the purpose. Pieces of unbleached muslin of heavy quality, measuring about 18 × 36 inches, edges left raw, and thoroughly boiled and rinsed to remove all dressing, will be found very satisfactory.

A **pan** for water in which to wet the press cloths is another helpful aid. This should be quite shallow with a wide top for ease in using and should have a capacity of about 2 quarts.

21. **Fitting Equipment.**—A certain amount of fitting equipment will be found very helpful in successful sewing. In fact, a *dress form*, so prepared as to duplicate your figure, is almost indispensable for the woman who sews for herself, while a *skirt gauge*, many types of which are available, will make for greater efficiency in marking the skirt length of garments.

THE SEWING MACHINE

HISTORY AND TYPES

22. The idea from which the modern sewing machine has developed originated in England in the 18th Century, but it was not until 1846 that Elias Howe, of Spencer, Massachusetts, made the sewing machine an invention of practical utility. Many experiments were conducted and many crude machines developed, with constantly increasing efficiency in operation and results, until at the present time, the modern sewing machine is a marvel of mechanical perfection. An indispensable aid to all who sew, it will give long years of usefulness, provided, of course, it is used intelligently and receives the proper care and treatment.

In selecting a sewing machine, go into the matter carefully, examining the various types that are on the market. When you have familiarized yourself with them, buy the one that is most suitable for your needs and that is the best you can afford to buy. There is no economy in buying a poor grade machine, for the initial expenditure will be quickly increased by frequent repairs.

Accompanying each machine is a book that tells how to operate it and take care of it and also explains how to use the attachments. If you don't have such a book, by all means get one from the dealer or the agency from whom you bought your machine so that you may learn all about the kind of sewing machine you intend to use. It is also possible at many of the agencies to receive personal instruction in the use of a sewing machine and its attachments.

There are two general types of sewing machines as regards the stitch they make, namely, the *lock-stitch* and the *chain-stitch*, the characteristics of which are explained here.

LOCK-STITCH MACHINE

23. Nature.—As its name implies, the lock-stitch machine uses two threads, the upper, or needle, thread, and the lower, or bobbin, thread. The needle, or upper, thread, passes from the spool, which is supported by the spool holder on the arm of the machine, through the tension and then through the eye of the needle. The under, or bobbin, thread, comes from the shuttle or bobbin. When the machine is in operation, the needle carries the upper thread down to loop around the under thread and thus forms a lock stitch.

24. Adjustment of Tension.—Because much of the appearance of stitching depends on the tension of the threads, it is most important that this detail be properly adjusted. It is well, therefore, before starting to stitch on a garment, to try out the stitch on two thicknesses of the material that you are going to use. When the tension is exactly correct, the lock which forms the stitch occurs just where the two thicknesses of the material meet, and a perfect stitch is formed. If it were possible to cut away a section of the material, the locking of the stitch would appear as shown in Fig. 4. If the tension of the upper thread is too tight or that of the under thread too loose, the thread will lie straight along the upper surface of the material and appear as in Fig. 5. If the under tension is too tight or the upper one too loose, the thread will lie straight on the under side of the material and appear as in Fig. 6.

When the appearance of the stitch shows that the tension is incorrect, the loosening or tightening of the screw that controls the upper tension will generally take care of the difficulty. Of course, a change can be made in the shuttle, or under, thread tension, but, as a rule, if this is correct when the machine is purchased, it will not need further adjustment, and because of the delicacy of the mechanism should usually be left undisturbed.

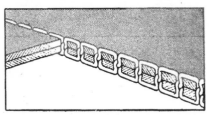

FIG. 4

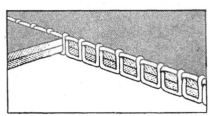

FIG. 5

25. Adjustment of Stitch.— Another important point to watch in lock-stitch machine stitching is the length of the stitch. When a stitch has been completed and before each succeeding stitch is commenced, the fabric that is being stitched is carried ahead by the feed mechanism, and on the length of its forward movement depends the length of the stitch. If this is too long or too short,

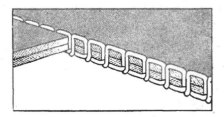

FIG. 6

the device that controls it should be adjusted. The material on which you are working determines the length of stitch to use. A rather small stitch generally looks best on silks and fine cottons and wools, while a longer stitch works to better advantage on the heavier weaves of wool and cotton. This detail, like the tension, should be adjusted before any stitching on the garment is done, by experimenting with a double thickness of the fabric to be used until the correct effect is obtained.

26. Ripping Lock-Stitching.—No instruction on lock-stitch machine sewing would be complete without information on ripping, for there is a correct way to rip just as there is a correct way to sew.

It is, of course, essential when ripping to remove all threads from the material, and the best way to do this is as follows : First, loosen one end of the upper thread by ripping a few stitches with a pin. Grasp this end firmly and pull until the thread breaks. Now, from the wrong side, grasp the under thread and pull until it breaks. Turn to the right side again, where you will find that there is generally a short length of thread loose, and repeat the process, alternating from one side to another until the stitching is all removed.

Another method of ripping uses a ripping knife or a safety razor blade. To rip in this way, cut the stitching between the two thicknesses of the material, holding the seam edges apart and cutting a little of the stitching at a time with the knife or blade. Such ripping requires great care to avoid cutting the material and also means that all loose threads must be picked or brushed out, a rather tedious process.

CHAIN-STITCH MACHINE

27. Nature.—The chain-stitch type of machine uses a single thread, which forms a stitch very similar to the lock-stitch on the right side, but is woven into a chain on the under side of the goods. This means that all of the stitching on a chain-stitch machine must be done on the right side of the fabric, and that great care must be taken in starting and finishing in order that the stitches may be securely fastened and the stitching not pull out. Such machines, however, are very easy to operate and provide a small fine even stitch that many women prefer. Chain-stitching may be ripped with very great ease by merely taking hold of the loose end and pulling. It is necessary, however, to begin to rip at the completed end of the stitching rather than the end at which the stitching was started.

CORRECT USE OF THE MACHINE

28. The instruction book that accompanies the sewing machine explains how to operate the various parts, so it should be studied thoroughly before you attempt to use the machine. In addition, it is important for you to become familiar with the information given here for certain points in connection with the machine as it will help you to make a success of whatever machine stitching you attempt to do.

29. Threading a Machine.—The first operation in the use of a machine is threading it. With the needle properly placed, the spool of thread on the spool holder, and the bobbin wound with thread and in place, thread the machine according to your sewing machine instruction book. Then pull the thread through the needle, hold the end of it in your left hand, and, with the right hand, turn the balance wheel until the needle goes down and comes up, bringing a loop of the under thread through the needle hole in the throat plate. Pull the end of the under thread into view and lay the ends of both threads back under the presser foot before starting to sew. This avoids knotting and lumping up of the thread at the beginning of the seam. Make sure that the slide covering the bobbin, or shuttle, is closed so that there will be no danger of tearing the material that is to be sewed.

30. Stitching.—Before attempting to sew, provided you are inexperienced, practice stitching on a piece of firm, smooth material, preferably striped, the stripes aiding you in keeping straight lines. Next, practice on plain cloth, striving always to keep a perfect line and the rows of stitching an equal distance apart. Also, practice stitching as close to an edge and as straight as possible.

Corners are very important and are best turned as follows : When the needle is exactly in the corner desired, raise the presser foot but do not raise the needle ; turn the material around the needle as a pivot ; lower the presser foot ; and begin to sew again. Never take a stitch unless the presser foot is down ; otherwise, the stitching will be loose and uneven.

In sewing, let the bulk of the work rest on the table at the left-hand side of the machine ; do not crowd it to the right of the presser foot, because then you cannot see the work so well, nor can you guide it evenly. Also, do not pull the cloth along when stitching, as this is liable to bend or break the needle or roughen the needle plate. The feed of the machine is intended to advance the work without assistance from the person who is doing the sewing.

31. Running a Machine.—In the operation of a sewing machine, as in that of any mechanical device, practice is necessary in order that the best results may be obtained. If you learn to sew on a foot-power machine, the proper motion of the feet must be mastered so that the machine will run with a motion that is smooth and regular as well as adapted to the type of sewing being done. This motion of the feet is entirely independent of the use of the hands and eyes, and so is sometimes difficult to put into practice. Nevertheless, experience will bring about expertness if much care is exercised in the running of the machine from the outset.

When using a sewing machine run by an electric motor, remember that the speed of the machine is regulated by the pressure exerted on the lever that controls it. The tendency of the beginner is toward too high speed, but every effort should be made to operate at a speed that will not be too rapid to produce good work. In fact, it is essential that the first practice be done slowly in order that just the right speed for good work may be acquired.

As a new operator, you must be careful, attentive, and painstaking. An easy, regular speed, not fast nor yet too slow, is best, not only for the machine but for you. Also, keep in mind the necessity of a gradual slowing up of speed as you approach the end of a seam or stitching line, for an abrupt stop jars the mechanism and puts an unwarranted strain on the various parts of the machine, especially in the case of the electrically driven type.

32. Machine Attachments.—All standard sewing machines are provided with a good assortment of attachments that are wonderful time savers and help to accomplish excellent results. To use them successfully, you must be able to stitch straight and even and understand the proper adjustment of each attachment. Some practice and thought are required before you will be proficient in the use of such attachments, but you can get the necessary help from the instruction book that accompanies your machine or from the local office of the sewing machine company.

33. Oiling and Caring for a Machine.—In oiling a sewing machine, drop oil into all places designated on the machine for oil, and place a little oil on parts that rub together. Insufficient oil makes the machine run hard, while if too much oil is used some is liable to drip on the material and form ugly spots.

If your sewing machine is in constant use, oil it sparingly every day and clean it every week. After each oiling, run the machine rapidly for a few moments, with the presser foot up, in order to work the oil into the bearings ; then wipe off the surplus oil carefully with a cloth that has been dipped in a cleaning fluid. Also, run the machine with the needle unthreaded over such a cloth.

No machine will run well if it is dirty with dust or oil ; neither will it run well if it is exposed to the air and allowed to rust. So, be very particular about keeping your machine clean. If, however, you have neglected this and it works very hard and squeaks, you may know that it is dirty and needs a thorough overhauling and cleaning. Follow the directions in your sewing machine book for adjusting the various parts and cleaning them. Often a thorough cleaning is all that is required to put in good condition a machine that is considered to be in need of repair. Just placing a little kerosene or benzine on the parts that rub together, running the machine rapidly for a minute or so, wiping all parts clean, and then oiling the machine will usually take care of the trouble. If, however, the cleaning and the methods of adjustment suggested in the instruction book fail to make the machine operate correctly, consult a sewing-machine repair man.

PRECAUTIONS IN USING THE SEWING MACHINE

34. Following is a summary of the precautions that should be observed in the operation of a sewing machine and the difficulties that sometimes occur in its use.

Avoid breaking needles by :

1. Using a good quality needle that is right for the machine.
2. Seeing that all attachments are securely fastened.
3. Using a needle right for the thread and material.
4. Letting the feed carry the work along without assistance.

If the *machine works heavily*, the trouble may be caused by :

1. Dust or lint clogging the working parts.
2. Insufficient oil.
3. Thread ends caught in the shuttle or bobbin case.

If the *needle thread breaks*, the trouble may be caused by :

1. Improper threading.	4. Needle blunt or set incorrectly.
2. Tight tension.	5. Presser foot not properly adjusted.
3. Thread too coarse.	6. Poor quality thread.

If the *bobbin or shuttle thread breaks*, the trouble may be :

1. Incorrect threading of bobbin. 3. Bobbin wound too tight.
2. Tight bobbin tension.   4. Bobbin wound too full.

If the *machine skips stitches*, the trouble may be caused by :

1. Needle improperly set.   3. Needle too fine for thread.
2. Needle blunt or bent.   4. Dust in the working parts.

If the *stitching puckers the material*, the trouble may be caused by :

1. Tight tensions.
2. Incorrect threading of the upper thread.
3. Too much or too little pressure on presser foot.

HAND AND MACHINE SEWING

PROCEDURE IN STUDYING

35. In passing on to the real work of making essential stitches and seams, you are again urged to study the text and illustrations in combination. In addition, you are advised to make the various stitches and seams as you proceed with the studies so that you may quickly acquire deftness with the needle. For this purpose, you should have on hand neatly pressed pieces of materials with which to make the *samplers*, as these samples of work are called. The samplers, for reasons of economy and convenience in handling, should correspond in size as nearly as possible with the actual illustrations. New materials can be used for this purpose if you desire, but as a rule small pieces taken from the scrap bag are satisfactory. In any case, however, the material should be cotton, preferably of a firm weave, and not too heavy quality. Lawn, gingham, or any similar fabric would be a good choice for this work, light or dark, as you prefer.

In many of the illustrations of sample stitches and seams, as you will observe, white thread is used on dark materials and dark thread on light materials. The sole reason for doing this is to bring out clearly the stitches and seams to the best advantage for study. Of course, in the actual work of sewing or in making samplers, you should use thread of the proper weight and quality for the material at hand and also pay due regard to colours, which should usually match as perfectly as possible but which may sometimes contrast for a desired effect.

THREADING A NEEDLE

36. The way in which to thread a needle is clearly illustrated in Fig. 7. Hold the needle between the thumb and the forefinger of the left hand and the thread between the thumb and the forefinger of the right hand, and insert the thread into the eye of the needle. To avoid tangling, put into the needle the end of the thread that first comes from the spool.

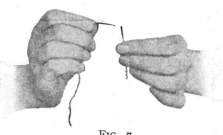

FIG. 7

Pull a little less than half the length through, and then tie a knot in the longer end by placing this end of the thread over the cushion of the forefinger of the left hand, holding it down with the thumb while bringing the thread around the finger and crossing it over the end of the thread, as shown in Fig. 8, then pushing the thumb down over the forefinger, twisting the thread, and finally pulling the knot down with the second finger. With a little practice, you can make a small, neat knot with ease.

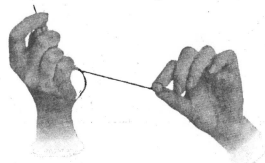

FIG. 8

When a larger knot is desired, tie two knots in the end as close together as possible. If you must sew with a double thread, bring the two ends together evenly and make a knot in them in the same way as directed for making a knot in a single thread, clipping off the thread ends if any extend beyond the knot.

In hand sewing, do not use a thread that is too long, because it is not only inconvenient to handle but also roughens up and often breaks because of the frequency with which it must be drawn through the material. From $\frac{1}{2}$ to $\frac{3}{4}$ yard of thread is plenty, except for basting, when you may use a longer thread for the stitches are longer in this case, and consequently there is not so much wear on the thread.

BASTING

37. Basting, which is not permanent sewing but which is used to hold the edges of material together until they are secured with finer stitches, is the first of all sewing operations. Even though it is all removed after the stitching that is to replace it is applied, it must be done carefully and generously if the article or garment is to be successfully completed.

There are three recognized types of basting, *even, uneven,* and *diagonal,* each of which has a definite use in sewing. To apply basting-stitches to material, regardless of the kind used, the method shown in Fig. 9 should be followed. First, pin together the two edges

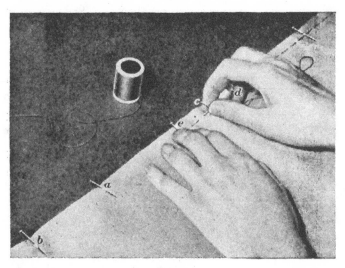

FIG. 9

to be joined, as at *a* and *b*, placing the pins at right angles to the seam edge; then, with the material laid flat on a table, start the basting at the right and work toward the left without raising the material away from the flat surface. As shown at *c*, hold the threaded needle between the thumb and forefinger of the right hand, and, with the thimble on the middle finger, as at *d*, push the needle with the aid of the thimble through the fabric along the seam line, usually ⅜ inch from the edge, taking two or three stitches at once. Notice that the left hand eases the material toward the right, as at *e*, thus making it easy for the needle to pick up the fabric. Baste right over the pins and, when the basting-stitches are placed, remove the pins.

38. Uneven basting is the most generally used form because of the ease and speed with which it may be accomplished. It is therefore discussed first. It is of two types, *regulation* and *dressmaker's*, and consists of alternating long and short stitches.

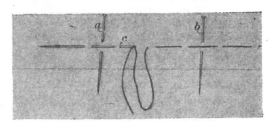

FIG. 10

39. To do *regulation, uneven basting*, pin the seam edges together as at *a* and *b*, Fig. 10 ; then, starting at the right with a knot, take a small stitch about ⅛ inch in length through both thicknesses of the material. Now skip a space of about ½ inch and take another stitch like the first. At *c* is shown the way to take these small stitches. Continue in this way, taking two or more stitches on the needle and working right over the pins, as shown, until the joining is made. Finish with two or more back-stitches to secure the end of the thread.

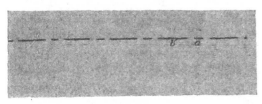

FIG. 11

40. Dressmaker's basting is clearly shown in Fig. 11. It consists of single long stitches followed by two short ones, and is found very satisfactory when a comparatively firm basted joining is needed. To accomplish it, take two ⅛-inch stitches with a ⅛-inch space between them, as at *a*, skip a space of ½ inch, as at *b*, and then repeat. Finish with two or more back-stitches.

41. Even basting, as shown in Fig. 12, consists of stitches that are the same length on the upper and under sides of the seam. Its uses are similar to those listed under uneven basting, but it is not quite so firm, particularly when the stitches are not taken very small. Make the stitches about ⅜ inch in

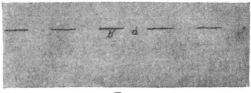

FIG. 12

length, as at *a*, and the spaces between the same length, as at *b*, continuing for the length of the seam and then fastening the thread.

42. **Diagonal basting** is of two types, *horizontal* and *vertical*, and is used to hold two pieces of material together, such as the two thicknesses of a collar, when more than one row of basting is needed. One

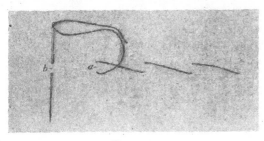

row of diagonal basting is equivalent to two of the straight type.

43. To do diagonal basting with *vertical stitches*, as s h o w n in Fig. 13, take a vertical stitch about ¼ inch long, as at *a*, then skip a space

FIG. 13

of about ¾ inch and take a second vertical stitch just like the first, as at *b*. Continue in this way to the end of the section being basted.

44. When diagonal basting is done with *horizontal stitches*, the process shown in Fig. 14 is followed. Take a straight horizontal stitch from right to left, about ½ inch long, as at *a*. Then insert the needle, as at *b*, ¾ inch above the first stitch and, for the diagonal effect, a slight distance back of where it first came out, and take the second stitch from *b* to *c*. Take the third stitch on the line with the first from *d* to *e*, inserting the needle at *d* slightly in front of the preceding upper one. Continue in this way, making all stitches the same length and having them as evenly spaced as possible.

MARK-STITCHES

45. **Mark-stitches,** or *tailor's tacks* as they are sometimes called, are illustrated in Fig. 15. Such stitches are not used to form a seam, but to mark pattern perforations and seam lines in materials in which tracing would be objectionable or would not show. In all dressmaking, mark-stitching is prac-

FIG. 14

tically indispensable for it is used to mark the location of darts, tucks, pleats, fullness, and so on, and in this way simplifies the making of any garment to a decided degree.

There are two types of mark-stitching, one made with a single stitch, and the other with a double stitch. The single-stitch mark-stitching can be accomplished more quickly, but has the disadvantage of pulling out more readily than the double-stitch type. It should be used, therefore, only when the garment is to be made up without delay ; otherwise, the mark-stitching might be lost.

Mark-stitching should be done after the garment is cut out, but before the pattern is removed from the material. The illustrations show the mark-stitching of an under-arm dart, but the same method should be followed for any feature of the garment. You will note that the pattern is pinned in place and the material is cut around all edges.

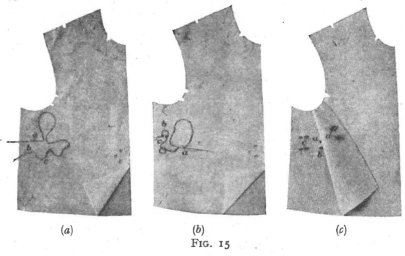

(a)   (b)   (c)

FIG. 15

46. To make mark-stitching of the *single-stitch* type, as shown in view (a), thread your needle with a double thread of contrasting colour and take a small stitch through both thicknesses of the material in the perforation, as at a, leaving a generous length of thread at the end, as at b. Now, take another stitch in the next perforation, leaving a loop between the two stitches, as at c. It is possible to skip from one perforation to the next when they are not too far removed from each other, as in the illustration ; but, when there is a great deal of space between them, it is better to clip the thread after each stitch, leaving the same length of thread at the end as at the beginning, and start again at each perforation. If, however, you have proceeded as shown here, clip the loops of thread left between each two stitches before attempting to remove the pattern.

47. To make the *double-stitch* type of mark-stitching, as shown in view (*b*), use double, contrasting thread in your needle, and take a stitch through both thicknesses of the fabric as directed for the single-stitch type. Then, just over the first stitch, take a back-stitch, as at *a*, leaving a loop in this, as at *b*. Skip to the next perforation and repeat. If the perforations are close together, the thread between them should be left loose, as at *c*, but if they are far apart the thead may be drawn smooth. Continue, until all perforations that indicate construction details have been marked ; then clip the threads where necessary, and remove the pattern.

For the final step, in both single and double-stitch mark-stitching, see that the pattern is removed and then prepare to cut the mark-stitching. To do this, separate the two thicknesses of material by pulling gently so that the loops of thread are drawn to the inside, as at *a* and *b*, view (*c*). Then clip through the centre of each loop, when the mark-stitches will appear as at *c* and *d*, marking both sides of your garment alike and aiding you in putting it together.

FOUNDATION NEEDLE STITCHES

48. The **running-stitch**, Fig. 16, is used for seams that require but little strength, for gathering or tucking, and in the construction of any garment in which hand work is employed.

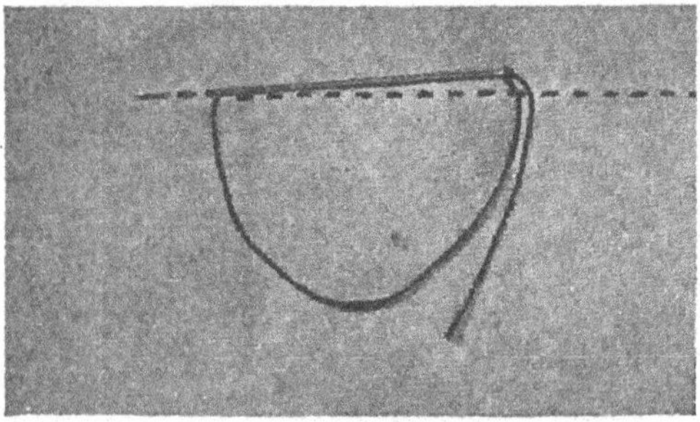

To make this stitch, hold the material between the thumb and first finger of both hands, insert the needle, and run it in and out until you have several tiny stitches of even length on it, guiding it between the thumb and first finger of the right hand and pushing it with the aid of the thimble on your middle finger. Then pull the needle through, take another needleful of similar stitches, and continue in this way. In most materials, the stitches may be made $\frac{1}{16}$ inch or less in length. Finish by taking two stitches back over the last running-stitch.

FIG. 16

49. **Back-stitching**, Fig. 17, is necessary where strength is needed and where machine stitching cannot be used.

To back-stitch, take first a very short stitch ; then bring the needle back, insert it at the point where you first placed it in the material, and bring it out the length of a very short running-stitch beyond the stitch just made, as at *a*. Make each stitch by putting the needle back into the end of the preceding stitch and bringing it out one stitch beyond, always advancing from the under side of the material. Back-stitching resembles machine stitching when carefully done. On the

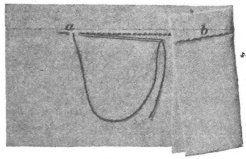

Fig. 17

wrong side, the stitches overlap, in the manner shown at *b*.

50. The **half-back-stitch**, Fig. 18, is sometimes used in joining seams or at points where less strength than that provided by back-stitching is necessary.

To make the half-back-stitch, take a stitch on the under side of the material twice as long as an ordinary running-stitch and proceed in much the same manner as in back-stitching ; but instead of bringing the needle back each time to the end of the preceding stitch, cover only half this distance, as at *a*. This stitch resembles the running-stitch, but is considerably stronger.

51. The **combination-stitch**, Fig. 19, can be made more quickly than back- or half-back stitching, and is often used where a little more strength than that given by a running-stitch is needed.

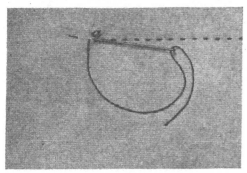

Fig. 18

To make the combination-stitch, first take three running-stitches ; then take one back-stitch and three more running-stitches, and continue in this way until the sewing line is complete. As shown in the illustration, the stitches, including the back-stitch on the right side, should be very small, that is, $\frac{1}{16}$ inch or less, if possible.

52. **Gathering,** Fig. 20, is made with small running-stitches, and the thread then drawn up to give the desired amount of fullness. To

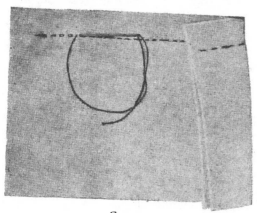

FIG. 19

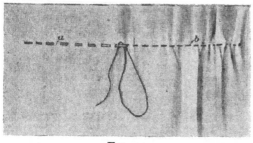

FIG. 20

FIG. 21

do gathering, use a fine needle and thread of corresponding size ; then, knot the thread and, starting at the right, take a number of stitches on your needle, as at *a*. Draw the needle through, pull up the thread to provide fullness in the part just gathered, as at *b*, and repeat until your stitches extend entirely across the space to be gathered. As an aid in adjusting the fullness evenly, a second row of gathering, $\frac{1}{8}$ to $\frac{1}{4}$ inch from the first, is often used. With the gathering-stitches in, adjust the fullness evenly and space it properly ; then fasten the thread securely with several back-stitches.

53. Overcasting, Fig. 21, is used to prevent the raw edge of a seam from ravelling.

To do overcasting, hold the raw seam edge over the finger, insert the needle in the seam edge deep enough to prevent ravelling, and take loose, slanting stitches over the single thickness of the edge, but not through to the right side of the garment, making these $\frac{1}{4}$ to $\frac{3}{8}$ inch apart and all of the same depth. Secure the thread by overcasting back over the last two or three stitches or by taking a few back-stitches.

After you have become thoroughly familiar with the overcasting - stitch, you may accomplish the work more quickly by taking several stitches on the needle at a time, as shown in Fig. 22. When a pressed-open seam is not essential, overcasting is frequently done over the two seam edges together, as this illustration shows, and a considerable saving of time effected in the finishing of a seam.

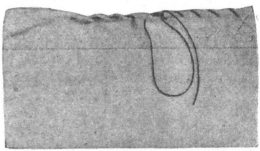

FIG. 22

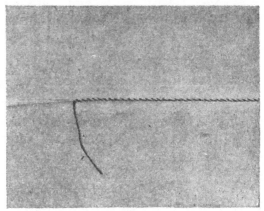

FIG. 23

54. Overhanding, Fig. 23, is used in joining two edges of material, usually selvages, where a flat seam is desired.

To do overhanding, proceed as follows : Baste the two edges together with the right sides of the material facing ; then hold the material in the left hand with the edges between the thumb and the forefinger ; place the needle in from the back and point it toward the left shoulder, picking up only a thread or two of each selvage or of each

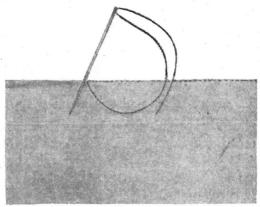

FIG. 24

turned edge, as in Fig. 24 ; take the stitches close together, over and over the edge, until the seam is completed. Be careful to make the stitches equal in length, not too tight, and just deep enough to catch the edges of the material so that when the overhanded seam is opened out it will lie perfectly flat and not form a cord or ridge. Finish the work the same as in overcasting.

55. The **catch-stitch**, Fig. 25, is used to finish seams flat or to hold an edge down securely, as when making up flannel for infants. The illustration shows catch-stitching applied to a plain pressed-open seam.

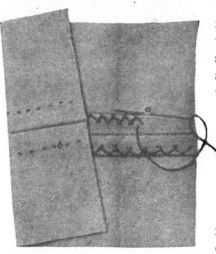

FIG. 25

To do this work, proceed as follows : Hold the seam so that the raw edge you wish to catch-stitch first is uppermost ; starting at the left, bring the needle out in this seam edge and take a tiny stitch just outside the seam edge, as at *a*. Then bring the needle down and to the right $\frac{1}{8}$ to $\frac{1}{4}$ inch, and take another tiny stitch in the seam edge, but not through to the right side, for, on the right side of the material, only one row of stitches should show on each side of the seam line, as at *b*.

Work from you, with the needle pointing toward the left shoulder each time, and continue the row of stitches, as shown. Take the last stitch in the seam edge and secure the work by taking two or three small stitches over this last stitch.

HEMMING AND HEMSTITCHING

56. A **hem** is an edge finish made by first turning up a narrow section of a raw edge, then making a second turn the determined hem width from the first, basting this in position, and finally securing the first turn. The depth of the first turn is usually from $\frac{1}{8}$ to $\frac{1}{4}$ inch while that of the second turn varies, depending on the type of material and the position of the hem. The securing of the hem may be done with any one of a number of different stitches, directions for which follow.

To make the **hemming**, as shown in Fig. 26, first bring the needle through the hem turn and then insert the needle from $\frac{1}{8}$ to $\frac{3}{16}$ inch away, as shown at *a*, picking up only a thread or two of the material and then catching the edge of the hem with a slanting stitch, as shown.

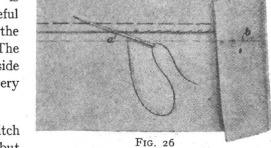

Repeat until the hem is completed, being careful not to draw any of the stitches too tight. The stitches on the right side will appear, as at *b*, very small and even.

FIG. 26

57. A hemming - stitch that is strong and firm but at the same time dainty and inconspicuous is the vertica hemming-stitch, as illustrated in Fig. 27. This kind of hemming takes its name from the direction of the stitches that hold the hem on the wrong side, as shown clearly in the illustration.

To do vertical hemming, first turn and baste the hem in the usual way. Next, bring the needle out through the hem turn, take a stitch just opposite the point where the needle comes out, taking up but one or two threads of the material, as at *a*, and then, a short distance beyond, inserting the needle in the hem close to the turned edge. Make the next stitch similar to the first, never drawing the thread tight but keeping an easy tension, and continue until the hem is completed. The stitches on the wrong side will appear straight up and down, as at *b*, while those on the right side will be horizontal, even, and small, as at *c*.

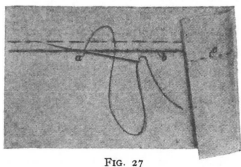

FIG. 27

58. The **napery** or **French** hem, shown in Fig. 28, is a strong, secure type of hem finish that lends itself to use on articles that are intended to give good service and also that require frequent laundering. It is, therefore, the ideal choice for table linen and towels.

To make the napery hem, turn and baste the hem in the usual way, and then crease on a line that meets the first fold of the hem, as at *a*. Hold the wrong side of the hem toward you and secure it in position by means of very small overhanding-stitches taken close together and quite taut, as at *b*. The stitches on the right side will appear straight, as at *c*, and will practically disappear into the material.

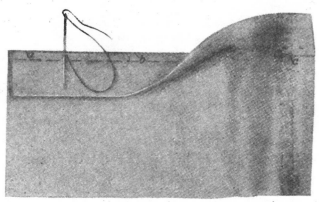

FIG. 28

59. The **slip-stitch,** or **blind-stitch,** is a method used in hemming or in fastening any turned edges where the stitches are to be as inconspicuous as possible. After first turning the hem the desired depth, baste it close to the edge, as at *a*, Fig. 29 ; then trim off the turned portion perfectly even and the desired width. Next, turn in the free edge a narrow seam's width and hold the turn with running-stitches, as at *b*, drawing up the thread enough for the hem to lie flat, provided the edge being hemmed is circular. On a straight hem, it will not be necessary for you to draw up the thread. Next, baste the hem to the garment close to its upper edge, as at *c*.

To slip-stitch, take a stitch in the hem edge by slipping the needle along the inside of the fold, as at *d*, and bringing it out about ¼ inch from where it entered ; then, take a stitch in the material to which the hem is to be fastened, taking up only a thread or two, as at *e*. Continue for the entire hem, being careful not to draw the slip-stitches tight. Then remove the bastings and press the hem well, dampening it slightly, if necessary, for a flat edge.

60. The **rolled, slip-stitched hem,** as shown in Fig. 30, is much used where a dainty finish is desired and is considered one of the representative forms of hand sewing. A certain skill, which must be developed by practice, is necessary for good results, but the time spent in acquiring this deftness is well worth while.

To make a successful rolled hem, the edge to be rolled must be free from ravellings ; therefore, trim off any frayed edges. Then, with the wrong side of the material toward you, roll the edge tightly between the thumb and forefinger of the left hand, taking care to keep an even edge and to make the roll as tight and tiny as possible, as at *a*. The tightness and size of the roll depend to a certain extent on the type of material being finished. Organdie, fine lawn, and similar

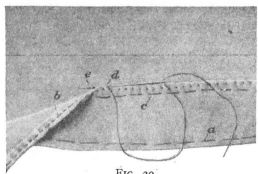

FIG. 29

fabrics, having a certain stiffness, can be rolled very readily, while naturally, any of the regulation dress fabrics whether silk or rayon, make a roll that is somewhat larger. After rolling enough of the edge to take the first stitch, secure the hem by fine slip-stitches, taking a stitch about ⅛ inch long in the roll, as at *b*, but merely picking up a thread or two of the material to which the rolled hem is to be fastened, as at *c*, so that the stitches will be practically invisible on the right side.

Continue in this way for the entire hem, rolling only a small portion at a time and placing the slip-stitches carefully as you advance.

61. Hand hemstitching, Fig. 31, is used as a substitute for hemming-stitches and as a simple trimming on straight edges for

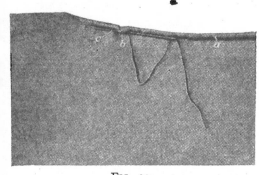

FIG. 30

household articles and certain items of apparel. The work consists in drawing, or pulling out, two or more parallel threads of the material and fastening the cross-threads in successive clusters, the procedure being as follows :

Measure in from the outside edge twice the width of the hem desired, plus the first hem turn, which is generally from ⅛ to ¼ inch wide ; draw as many threads of the material as desired, usually two to eight, depending on the material ; and then turn and crease the hem, basting it exactly along the line where the threads are drawn, as at *a*.

Using sewing thread and working from left to right with the wrong, or hem, side toward you, conceal the knot in the hem, hold the thread at the left under the left thumb, and take up three to six threads on the needle, as shown at *b*, by inserting the needle at the right of the threads and bringing it out at the left and *over*

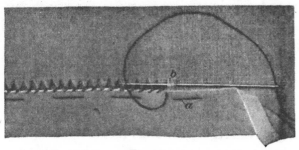

FIG. 31

the thread from the needle, as shown.   The number of threads to take up will depend on the material and whether you wish the hemstitching coarse or fine.   Draw the stitch up firmly but not too tight, thus grouping the threads together.   Pull the thread down toward the hem in doing this.   Then take a whipping-stitch to the right of the group of threads, catching one or two threads in the material next to the drawn space and two or three on the turn of the hem and letting the needle come out *under* the thread.   Repeat these two stitches alternately for the distance required.   Right and wrong sides are practically alike in appearance.

FOUNDATION SEAMS

62.   The word **seam** is the term applied to the joining of two sections of an article or garment.   There are several types of seams, the kind to use depending on the fabric, the design of the garment, and Fashion.   The various kinds of seams are explained and illustrated in the following articles.

63.   The **plain seam,** Fig. 32, is the simplest of all seams and the one most frequently used in dressmaking.   It is easy to make, inconspicuous in effect, and appropriate for most materials and for joinings that are not too intricate or curved.

To make a plain seam, place the right sides of the material together with the seam lines meeting, pin, and baste. Stitch as near the basting line as possible, as at *a*, remove the basting-threads, and press the seam edges open, as at *b*.

64. The **French seam,** Fig. 33, is really a double seam, stitched twice and having all raw edges covered. It is most valuable as a finish on garments that require frequent laundering, such as lingerie and children's wear

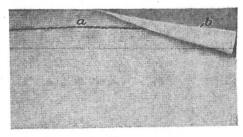

Fig. 32

and on fine sheer fabrics whose transparency allows the seam finish to show through. It is not appropriate for definitely curved nor intricate shaped joinings nor for heavy fabrics.

To make a French seam, pin together the two seam edges that are to be sewed, having the seam come to the right side; baste on the seam line; stitch a scant ¼ inch outside the basted line; remove the basting; trim off the frayed edge to within a scant ⅛ inch of the first stitching, and press the seam edges together to one side. Next, reverse the material so that the right sides come together and the raw edges are between them, as at *a*, Fig. 33, crease exactly on the stitched line, baste on the seam line, and then stitch, as at *b*. This row of stitch-ing must fully cover the edges of the previous seam, thus explaining why it is necessary to trim all frayed edges from the first seam.

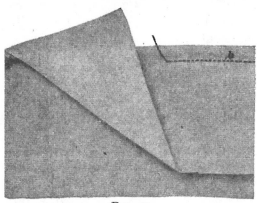

Fig. 33

For materials that fray or stretch easily, it may be necessary to allow ½ to ⅝ inch for the seam, and make the first row of stitching a little farther from the seam line.

In very sheer materials, where the seaming is done by hand with the combination-stitch, a dainty seam ⅛ inch or even less in width may be made; in such cases, however, do not overlook the importance of having the second seam large enough to cover the first entirely, nor of having the last stitching exactly in the seam line.

65. The **fell**, another type of seam that conceals all raw edges, is of two varieties, the *flat fell* and the *standing*, or *French, fell*. The **flat fell**, Fig. 34, is a flat seam made with two stitchings, both of which usually appear on the right side of the garment, although either side of the seam may be considered the right side depending on the manner in which it is used. It is a sturdy finish for sports wear, undergarments, and household sewing.

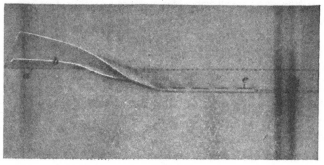

FIG. 34

To make a flat-fell seam, place the edges of the material together, pin, baste, and stitch, as at *a*, as for a plain seam, having the seam allowance on the right side if both stitchings are to appear on this side. Then, press the seam flat, to one side, trim off the under edge to ⅛ inch of the stitching, as at *b*, turn the other edge under ⅛ inch, baste to the garment, as at *c*, and stitch, as at *d*.

66. The **standing**, or **French, fell**, Fig. 35, is, as its name indicates, a combination of the fell and French seams. It provides a practical joining where the inside seams of the garment must have no raw edges, and is, therefore, much used on transparent fabrics such as organdies and chiffons, as well as undergarments and children's clothes. It is an especially good finish where straight and gathered edges must be joined, as in the application of a ruffle.

To make a standing fell seam, pin, with right sides together, the edges to be joined, baste, and then stitch them, as at *a*, Fig. 35, view (*a*), using the usual ⅜-inch seam allowance. Press the seam. Trim away one seam edge to within 1/16 to ⅛ inch of the stitching, as at *b*, turn in the free edge ⅛ inch, as at *c*, and baste it in place to the seam allowance, as at *d*, so that the edge just covers the stitching. Whip this edge to the stitching, as at *e*, or machine-stitch it.

Another method, which requires only one stitching, is shown in view (*b*). To make this, pin, then baste the edges together, as at *a* having the seam on the wrong side. Trim off one edge to within

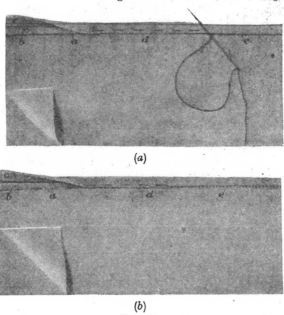

(*a*)

(*b*)

Fig. 35

$\frac{1}{16}$ to $\frac{1}{8}$ inch of the basting, as at *b*, turn in the free edge $\frac{1}{8}$ inch, as at *c*, baste so that the turn just covers the first basting, as at *d*, and stitch, as at *e*, when a standing seam will be the result.

67. The **overlapped seam** is a very satisfactory method of making a joining that is irregular in shape or one in which it is desired to place a certain emphasis on the seam. In fact, this particular variety of seam is much used in modern dressmaking and tailoring on almost all types of materials.

To make the overlapped seam, first determine which edge is to be on top. As a rule, the skirt section of a garment laps over the waist section. A yoke, whether it occurs in the waist or in the skirt, would lap over the section to which it is to be joined. An inserted or applied section, however, is generally lapped over the section in which it is inserted. Turn in a seam's width the edge that is to be lapped over the other and baste, as at *a*, Fig. 36. At the outward turning points, fold the excess material neatly into a mitre, as at *b*. At the inward turning ones, clip the seam allowance to within $\frac{1}{16}$ to $\frac{1}{32}$ of an inch of the turn, as at *c*. If the material is

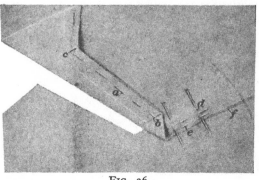

soft and frays readily, do not clip too close; the firmer fabrics, on the other hand, require less of an allowance at the point. Around a curve that extends into the material, clip the edge to permit the turn to lie flat, while around an outward extending curve, ease in the excess

FIG. 36

as you baste. Be careful, when basting, neither to stretch nor tighten the edge, as the finished seam must be flat and smooth for a professional effect.

When one edge is turned and basted, place it over the other to which it is to be joined, lap it a seam's width, and pin at right angles to the seam, as at *d*, placing the pins from 1 to 1½ inches apart. Baste, as at *e*, and then replace the basting with stitching close to the turned edge, as at *f*.

BUTTONHOLES

68. A **buttonhole** is a slit made in a garment to receive a button, and since it affords a very satisfactory method of fastening, it should by all means be made correctly. The foundation for a buttonhole should consist of two or more thicknesses of material, depending on the nature of the fabric. If buttonholes are desired in a single thickness, a scrap of the material should be basted under the line marked for the buttonhole, the buttonhole worked through two thicknesses, and the underneath material then trimmed away close to the buttonhole-stitches.

69. A *horizontal buttonhole* is one that runs crosswise, as in Fig. 37. As a rule, it should be used where there is any strain, such as at the neck line of a child's dress, in play suits, rompers, housecoats, tailored cuffs, as well as undergarments.

A *vertical buttonhole* is one that runs up and down, as shown in Fig. 38. It is used for the front closing of a man's shirt or boy's blouse or a tailored or lingerie shirtwaist. Full-length dress closings, when finished with worked buttonholes, often use the vertical type.

70. Marking for Buttonholes.—In marking for buttonholes, measure from top to bottom the length of the space in which the buttonholes are to be placed, so as to determine how many buttons and buttonholes will be needed. Place pins to indicate the location of the first and last buttonholes. Then divide the space between them by one more than the remaining buttonholes to be located, and

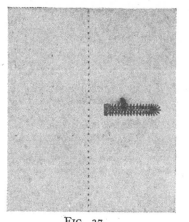

FIG. 37

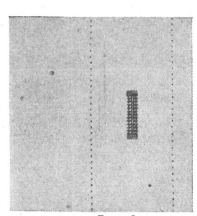

FIG. 38

place a pin at each division point to mark the location of a button-hole. For instance, if you wish to place 5 buttons in a 7½-inch space, divide 7½ by 6 and you get 1¼, or the number of inches between the buttonholes.

71. Cutting Buttonholes.—For cutting buttonholes, sharp scissors as well as a steady hand are essential, for much of the success of the finished buttonhole depends on the trim manner in which it is cut. Practice in cutting is helpful. If possible, cut horizontal button-holes on a crosswise thread of any fabric and vertical buttonholes on a lengthwise thread, and in each instance cut the buttonhole from 1⁄16 to ¼ inch larger than the button itself, a thick button requir-ing a larger buttonhole than a thin one. To prevent fraying, cut each buttonhole as you are ready to work it, instead of cutting all the buttonholes at one time.

72. Before using buttonhole scissors in cutting buttonholes, adjust them and try them on a scrap of material; then slip one of

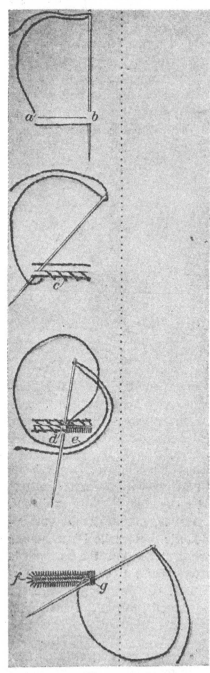

FIG. 39

the buttons through the slit to test its size, having it slightly loose as it will tighten somewhat in the working.

If you use regular scissors in cutting the buttonholes, first mark the length of the buttonhole with a pencil and insert a pin at one end of the mark. Then fold the material through the centre of the marked buttonhole line, having the fold exactly on a straight thread of the fabric, and insert the pin at the other end of the line. Cut through the four thicknesses of material from the fold to the pin, which will permit the scissors to cut only so far.

In materials that fray readily, you will find it advantageous, before cutting the buttonholes, to stitch, by hand or machine, $\frac{1}{16}$ inch or a trifle less on each side of the lines on which the buttonholes are to be cut. The stitching will give firmness and help to keep the stitches even.

73. Stranding Buttonholes. First, to prevent the edges from stretching and also to make the buttonhole firm, supply what is known as a *stranding thread* by bringing the needle out just below the inner end of the buttonhole, taking a small back stitch to make the thread secure, and then taking a short stitch under the opposite,

or outside, end, as at *a*, bringing the needle back, and taking a small'
stitch under the inner end, or at the point from which you started,
as at *b*. By doing this, you will form two stitches that lie close
to the buttonhole opening and are equal in length to this opening.
Draw these stranding stitches close, but not so tight as to cause
the buttonhole to pucker.

74. Overcasting Buttonholes.—Next, to hold the stranding
threads in position and also to prevent the edges of the buttonhole
from fraying, take a few overcasting stitches over them, as at *c*,
continuing with the same thread that you used in stranding. Stranding and overcasting are very often omitted in the making of buttonholes, but as these details are of so much value in insuring neat
and substantial results, they should receive consideration, especially
until skill has been attained in the work.

75. Working Buttonholes.—After completing the overcasting,
bring this same thread out about $\frac{1}{16}$ inch below the inner end of
the opening in preparation for working the buttonhole-stitch. To
make this stitch, with the outer edge of the garment at the left,
place the buttonhole opening over the forefinger of the left hand
and hold it in position with the thumb ; insert the needle through the
slit and then in the edge of the buttonhole, as at *d*, to make a short
stitch, usually about $\frac{1}{16}$ inch deep ; bring the threads that come from
the eye of the needle around under the point of the needle to the
left forming a loop, as at *e*, and then draw up the thread firm and
close, but not tight enough to draw the edges apart. A stitch made
in this manner forms a *double purl* at the edge of the buttonhole ;
this makes a firmer and more durable finish than the single purl of
the blanket-stitch.

Continue working the buttonhole-stitches across the lower edge
of the buttonhole, making them close together and all of the same
length, as the illustration shows. When you reach the outer end,
take several buttonhole-stitches around it, spacing them evenly,
as at *f*, and making these stitches somewhat deeper than those along
the edge, thus forming what is known as a *round end* or *fan finish*.
Such a finish is especially desirable for a buttonhole in which there
is a decided strain at the end, for besides being very firm it affords
a resting place for the button.

Next, turn the work so that the upper edge of the buttonhole is
next to you and continue making buttonhole stitches of equal depth.

76. Piecing the Thread.—If the thread you are using for the buttonhole breaks or you find that the thread is not long enough to complete the work, you may dispose of the end of this thread by taking a few very fine running-stitches along the under side of the buttonhole-stitches that have been worked, taking care, however, not to let these running-stitches show on the right side. Do not cut off the end of the thread until after you complete the buttonhole, however.

To start the new thread, take a few running-stitches from the opposite direction along the unfinished edge, leaving the end of the thread free so that it may afterwards be drawn tight, if necessary, and bring the needle out in the purl of the last buttonhole-stitch that was worked. Then proceed with the making of the buttonhole-stitches, working over, and thus concealing the running-stitches that started the new thread. A piecing made in this manner will not be at all noticeable.

77. Making Buttonhole Bar.—When you reach the inner end of the buttonhole, finish this with a *bar*, as at *g*, by taking several stranding stitches across this end and then working over them with single-purl stitches by bringing the needle out over the thread, the same as in making the blanket-stitch. Place these stitches close together, so that they will entirely conceal the stitches underneath, and catch several of them through the material so as to make the bar firm.

Finish the buttonhole by taking a couple of tiny back-stitches on the wrong side, and if you have made a piecing in the thread, draw the ends a trifle so as to tighten the stitches and then clip them close to the material.

78. Working Vertical Buttonholes.— To make a vertical button-hole, follow practically the same method as in making a horizontal buttonhole, but as the round end, or fan finish, is not required as a resting place for the button, finish both ends of the buttonhole with bars, thus giving a uniform appearance.

79. Sewing on Buttons.—Special methods must be followed in applying buttons for good results. The buttonhole will fit smoothly under the correctly sewed-on button and will give the appearance of trim neatness that should be characteristic of all fastenings.

When preparing to sew on buttons, first mark the position for each button by lapping the garment properly and then bringing a pin up from underneath to the side on which the buttons are to be sewed, directly through the centre of each buttonhole. Take care that both sides of the garment are perfectly smooth, so that the space between the buttons will correspond with that between the buttonholes.

(a)

80. To sew on a *two-hole button*, use double thread of a colour to match the garment or the button, and, when possible, of a heavy quality, and insert the needle from the right side at the point marked by the pin so that the knot of the thread will be on the same side of the material as the button and directly underneath it. Now, bring the thread up through to the right side, insert the needle through one hole of the button, and put it down through the other hole and through the material. With the one stitch made, put a pin or two across the button underneath the loop of thread, as shown at *a*, Fig. 40, view (*a*), to prevent the button from being sewed too close to the garment and to provide a thread shank so that the buttonhole side of the garment will lie flat and smooth around the buttons. If the material is heavy, such as might be the case with linen, wool, or wool suitings and coatings, use an article thicker than a pin, such as a match stick, an orange stick, a knitting needle, or a fine stiletto, which, because of their greater circumference, will make the loops of thread for the shank long enough to fit over the greater thickness of material.

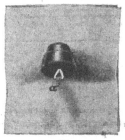
(b)

Sew back and forth until a sufficient number of threads have been placed, bring the needle out between the material and the button, remove the pins, draw the button away from the material as far as possible, and wind the thread as it comes out of the material around the thread shank, keeping it tight and smooth, as at *b*. Now, bring the needle to the wrong side and fasten the thread securely with

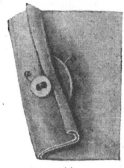
(c)

FIG. 40

back-stitches. If your buttons are to be quite close together, do not cut the thread but carry it on the under side from one button to the next.

81. To sew on a *four-hole button*, follow the method just described but bring the needle up and down through the four holes the same number of times, either criss-crossing the threads or running them parallel, the parallel threads being preferred when working with tailored wear and the criss-cross threads giving a strong finish for work garments, children's play clothes, and so on.

82. To sew on a *shank button*, proceed as shown in view (*b*), running the stitches through the shank, as at *a*, and parallel to the edge of the garment as the strain will then fall on the shank rather than on the thread. Take as many stitches as are necessary for a secure fastening.

83. To sew on a *reinforced button*, that is, a button reinforced on the wrong side by a tiny button, such as would be used on men's and boys' overcoats and sports dresses and coats for women and children, follow the plan shown in view (*c*). Take the first stitch in the right side of the garment at the proper location, and then bring the needle out on the wrong side through one hole of the small button *a*, which has been placed in the correct location on the wrong side, and run it up through the other hole to the right side. Run the needle up and down through the holes of the large button *b*, form the shank or stem with pins or a stiletto, and then continue taking stitches through both buttons at the same time until a sufficient number of threads have been placed. Remove the pins, draw the top button out smoothly, and wind the shank. Fasten the thread with several back-stitches on the wrong side between the small button and the fabric.

ESSENTIAL STITCHES AND SEAMS

EXAMINATION QUESTIONS

(1)   What equipment is essential for the beginner in sewing ?

(2)   Why is pressing equipment important ?

(3)   (a) What determines the length of the stitch to use in machine sewing ? (b) When and how should the tension and stitch be adjusted ?

(4)   How many kinds of basting are there, and what are their uses ?

(5)   What is the purpose of mark-stitching ?

(6)   Why should the frayed edges of a French seam be trimmed away before the last stitching is done ?

(7)   Describe the two fell seams.

(8)   How much larger should a buttonhole be than the button that is to be used with it ?

(9)   Send to us for inspection a sampler of overcasting, as shown in Fig. 21.

(10)   Send for inspection a sampler of the napery hem, Fig. 28.

(11)   Send us a sampler of the slip-stitch, as in Fig. 29.

(12)   Send a sampler of hand hemstitching, as shown in Fig. 31.

(13)   Send for inspection a sampler of the French seam shown in Fig. 33.

(14)   Send a sampler of an overlapped seam shaped as in Fig. 36.

EASY GARMENT MAKING

HELPFULNESS OF SEWING

1. Next in importance to knowing how to make the stitches and seams used in sewing is the ability to apply such knowledge ; that is, to be able to cut out materials and to make garments. You will find sewing not only pleasant work, but work that will enable you to increase your self-reliance, and once you realize its opportunities, possibilities, and advantages, every hour you spend at it, provided you do the work conscientiously, will mean pleasure and profit to you.

To develop any garment successfully, you must draw upon your imagination and see before you the finished product, perfect in every line and stitch ; then you should strive to duplicate your mental picture. The success of the garments you make will depend on your earnestness, on the skill with which you use the actual tools of your craft, and on your faculties and your ability to apply them.

2. As a beginner in sewing, you are not expected to possess all the essential qualities of a successful dressmaker, but as your skill in sewing increases, so will your vision and knowledge broaden. And the knowledge you acquire will be a help to economy, for it will aid you both in cultivating the taste for better things in dress and in satisfying that taste ; also, when you can sew well, it will enable you to have more clothes of better material, workmanship, and style than a limited knowledge of sewing would permit.

3. Getting Results From Practical Work.—The ideal plan by which the art of dressmaking may be mastered, consists of a proper blending of study and practice work. Therefore, at this time, a group of attractive, and, at the same time, practical and simply made garments, is presented, these to be cut direct from the fabric or with the aid of patterns which you will develop yourself. It is well for you to make all of these garments, in order to gain valuable experience.

If this is not possible, however, read over very carefully the instructions relative to the making of them and work out by means of a sampler any feature of construction that seems difficult. Such practice will give you a much better understanding of the text as well as valuable experience.

At the very beginning, it is essential that you approach your sewing in the proper frame of mind, that is, with the determination to strive for perfection and success, for, if every one of the points of construction described in the following pages is completely mastered by you at this time, you will have laid a worth-while foundation for all of the future work you do. Then, too, there is every reason to believe that if you interpret the instructions properly and apply them correctly, you will be proud to wear any of the garments recommended for making. So, select colours and fabrics for becomingness as well as practical appeal.

Keep in mind, also, that speed is not essential at this time. Thoughtful care given to every item of your work from the placing of the first pin to the removal of the last basting thread will mean much to you now. Later on, as your skill increases, the time you require to make a garment will decrease in proportion.

4. Helpful Suggestions.—Some provision must, of course, be made for cutting, because lack of a sizable surface will be found a serious handicap. The simplest solution of the problem is a section of wall board or similar material that can be placed on a table or even on a bed. Such a cutting surface is flat and smooth, it is light in weight but firm, and will save wear and tear on a table that might ordinarily be used for this purpose.

You will also need a well-sharpened pencil, tailor's chalk, a ruler, a yard-stick, and a tape measure. Pins in generous quantity and shears of the proper size are, of course, essentials. In the directions that follow, when working on a fabric, use pins and tailor's chalk for the markings; if you are forming a paper pattern, use your pencil, as directed.

Measurements naturally are very important ; therefore, take them carefully, just as directed. When the figure is not exactly in proportion, however, it is suggested that you use proportionate measurements and then take care of any necessary adjustments during fitting. Such a plan will enable you to obtain more satisfactory patterns because they will be in the correct balance.

GARMENT CONSTRUCTION

SIMPLE APRONS

MAGIC APRON

5. The first garment to be considered here is the Magic Apron shown in Fig. 1, so simple that it can be made as if by magic. An apron is a garment that is very desirable for all home girls and women, and, as the particular style illustrated is practical and easily made, it not only fills an actual need, but through its development affords excellent practice work and an opportunity to become familiar with elementary garment construction.

The apron consists simply of a skirt with bib, a bib strap, a belt, and two pockets. Blanket-stitching in a contrasting colour finishes the edges of the bib and the top of the pockets, providing a touch of hand-work that can be quickly done and that adds greatly to the finished appearance of the apron. Such materials as calico, percale, and gingham are suitable for its development, and only one length, or, for the average figure, about 1⅛ yards of material, will be required for it. No pattern is needed for this apron.

6. Knowing Your Material.—Familiarity with the quality of the material you are going to use, its weave, texture, pattern, and possibilities, is an essential feature, for cutting is often unsuccessful merely because the fabric being cut is not thoroughly understood. For this apron, the first garment you make, select a material of even weave and firm texture, provide the amount needed, and then examine it carefully. Look at the design first, if there is one, and determine whether or not it has an up-and-down effect, as is sometimes the case with floral motifs, bow-knots, or other naturalistic prints, and, at times, with conventional designs as well. If you find that your material has such a feature, place it for cutting so that the top of each motif is toward the top of the article or garment being made.

Next, examine closely the threads that go to make up the weave, the lengthwise threads being those which are parallel to the selvage, that is, run in the same direction, and the crosswise threads being

those at right angles to the selvage. Learn to follow these threads with the eyes, for in all dressmaking, it is very important that the thread of the material be understood and its significance thoroughly appreciated. In fact, no garment can be properly constructed if the grain or thread of the fabric in relation to the garment is ignored.

In this case, examine the lengthwise fold in your material, if there is one, to see whether it is exactly on a lengthwise thread, since this fold is to represent the centre front of the apron and naturally must be straight or the entire apron will neither look well nor set well. If the fold does not follow a straight thread, press out the crease completely and refold the material exactly on a lengthwise thread. This instruction can be applied to any garment that contains a certain section or sections intended to be cut along the straight thread of the lengthwise fold.

7. Cutting Out the Apron.—To provide for the strap, belt, and one of the pockets, trim off a 6-inch strip from the apron material from selvage to selvage on a straight thread of the

FIG. 1   fabric. From one end of this strip,

cut a section 5½ inches long for one of the pockets; cut the part remaining through the centre to form two bands, each 3 inches wide.

Make sure that both ends of your material are straight; then, with it folded through the lengthwise centre, place it on a table with the fold nearest you, as shown in Fig. 2. Considering the corner at the lower right *a*, measure from this point along the cut edges a distance equal to one-half the bib width and call this point *b*, this being 4 inches for the medium, 3 to 3½ for the small, and 4½ to 5 inches for the large figure. Now, to the left of *a*, measure the bib length and consider this point *c*. This also will vary with size, 9 inches being a

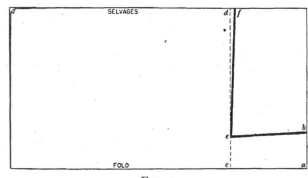

FIG. 2

suitable amount for the medium, 7 to 8 inches for the short, and 10 inches for the tall figure. Straight up from *c*, mark a line with pins or tailor's chalk to the selvage edges, and call its end *d*. On this line, locate *e* as a point to indicate the width of the bib at the waist line, having the distance from *c* to *e* ½ inch less than from *a* to *b*, that is, 3½ inches for the medium, 2½ to 3 inches for the small, and 4 to 4½ inches for the large figure. Join *b* and *e* with tailor's chalk or a row of pins to guide you in cutting. From point *d*, measure to the right ½ inch and call this point *f*; then join *e* and *f* with a line of pins, thus providing a slight slant for the waist-line edges. With these points indicated, cut from *b* to *e* and from *e* to *f* along the marked lines.

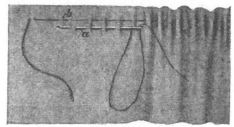

FIG. 3

8. Arranging the Fullness.—The first step in the making of the apron is the arrangement of the fullness at the sides. This is done by means of gathering. For this process, use a medium fine needle and a single thread of moderate length and weight, generally number 50, that matches your material, unless it is very light in colour, when white is permissible. Knot the long end of the thread, and then, starting at the right hand end, take a number of very fine

FIG. 4

running-stitches on the needle $\frac{1}{4}$ inch from the edge, as at a, Fig. 3, draw up the thread, take another needleful of running-stitches, and continue in this manner until you reach a point within $\frac{1}{2}$ inch of the bib. Now, remove the thread from the needle, leaving the end free and tying a knot in it if it seems so short that it might slip back through the material. The work at this stage will appear as at b.

In order to be able to arrange the gathers easily and evenly when applying the waist band, a second row of shirring is placed below the first and about $\frac{1}{8}$ inch from it. Follow exactly the same process as that suggested for the first row, taking care to have the stitches exactly in line with those already taken, that is, each stitch in the lower row exactly under a corresponding stitch in the upper row. Finish the end of the thread with a knot. You will find this plan a satisfactory one to follow in practically all the gathering you do, particularly when a gathered edge is being applied to a plain one. Now, draw up both threads to the same degree of tautness, and then arrange the fullness evenly over the required amount of space, as at c. This will usually be about 8 inches for the medium figure, 6 inches for the small, and 10 inches for the large. Gather the other side in the same manner, taking the first gathering-stitch $\frac{1}{2}$ inch from the bib and placing the first row of gathers $\frac{1}{4}$ inch from the edge and the second row $\frac{1}{8}$ inch from the first, as on the other side.

FIG. 5

9. Finishing the Waist Line.—The waist bands are the next to be finished. If you are slender, you may require only the length in each band that can be had by cutting into two sections one of the strips allowed for the purpose, each 3 inches wide and about 13 to 15 inches long, depending on the width of the material you are using. If, after measuring the length of the bands plus the width of the bib at its widest point, you find that you need more length in order that the apron may rest easily at a becoming waist line when the waistband is fastened, cut two strips 3 inches wide and the required length from the material remaining beyond the bib, indicated by the lines *b e* and *e f* in the diagram, Fig. 2, and join one of these to each of the longer strips in a plain seam. Press the seams open.

FIG. 6

Next, turn and baste the ends of each band in a ¼-inch turn, then baste the band to the gathered section of the apron, as shown at *a*, Fig. 4, with the right side of the band to the wrong side of the apron and one of the turned ends, as at *b*, next to the bib. Keep the gathers even, also keep the gathered section the determined length, not allowing the gathers to spread. Then baste the ¼-inch turn around the rest of the band, as shown. Try the apron on to see whether the skirt part comes back far enough to look well, keeping in mind that, to be serviceable, an apron should be a real protection to the dress over which it is worn.

Measure at this time, also, the length you will need for the bib strap, by pinning the bib to the dress in the desired position and measuring from one upper corner around the neck to the other corner, allowing about 1 inch excess length. Do not make the mistake of having this measurement too short, for much of the comfort of wearing the apron depends on having the waist line a snug fit and the bib strap long enough not to pull across the back of the neck.

Make any necessary changes in the position of the gathers either by drawing them up or by spreading them apart, replacing the ripped basting-threads first with pins and then with bastings when the apron has been removed.

FIG. 7

10. Finishing the Bib.—In order to have the hem of the bib lie flat for its entire length, it is necessary to clip in a seam's width at that place where the bib and the apron meet. To do this, cut in ¼ inch, or the width of the first hem turn, at right angles to the edge of the bib section, as shown at *c*, Fig. 4.

Now bring the waist band over to the right side and baste it in place, as at *a*, Fig. 5. Then turn the bib hem and baste it in place, as at *b*. Bring the hem *b* over the end of the waist band on the right side so that the material at *c* forms a pleat and the inner edge of the hem is in line with the end of the waist band on the wrong side, as at *a*, Fig. 6, the pleat below the band being indicated by *b*. Baste in position, as shown at *c*. Now turn the apron to the right side and begin to stitch at a point corresponding to *d* so that the stitching comes just along the edge of the bib ; turn at the corner, and continue the stitching along the edge of the waist band, as at *e*, catching all edges of the waist band on the right as well as the wrong side, and stitching between the two rows of gathering.

11. Before finishing the bib, prepare the strap, lengthening the band allowed for this purpose, if necessary, by piecing it with a strip of the same width cut from the section *b e f*, Fig. 2. With the strap the proper length, fold it through the centre lengthwise, right sides in, stitch a ¼-inch seam along the long edge and across one end, and turn the strap right side out. An easy way to do this is to place the blunt end of a pencil against the end seam and pull the strap down over the pencil, as in Fig. 7, until it is completely turned. Then slip out the pencil, baste the strap flat with the seam on the edge, first squaring the corners of the stitched end, and press. Turn back the raw end of the strap about ¼ inch, and baste the strap in place, just at the corners of the bib, with the raw edges concealed.

In order to make the strap more comfortable around the back neck line, find the exact centre of its length on the wrong side and fold on the centre line. Place a line of basting inside this fold, having it ½ inch from the inside, or top, edge and tapering it to nothing at the outside, or lower, edge, and replace with stitching, tying the ends of the threads securely. This shaping will cause the strap to lie flat and help to prevent any tendency to draw.

12. You are now ready to do the blanket-stitching. Thread the needle with single-strand embroidery floss of a medium weight in fast-colour black or a harmonizing colour, fasten the thread on the wrong side, and bring the needle up through the bib at *a*, Fig. 8, so that the work may be commenced at this point. Insert the needle through the bib just over the line of basting that holds the hem, as shown, and bring it out very close to point *a* under the hem and over the loop formed by the thread, as at *b*. Draw up the thread to form

what is known as a *single purl*. The stitches up to the top of the
waist band should be taken through all thicknesses of material to
keep the edges flat. Continue the blanket-stitching around the
bib, placing each stitch just outside the edge of the hem turn and
keeping the stitches an even distance apart,
as at *c*. At each of the corners, take the
blanket-stitches through the shoulder strap
to secure the ends.

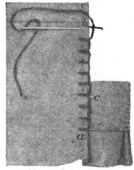

If you have never done blanket-stitching
before, put a little time in practice in order
that you may do good work on your apron.

13. Hemming the Apron.—Turn and baste
a hem on the lower edge, as at *a*, Fig. 9,
making it 2½ to 3 inches deep. Then, stitch
the hem in position, starting at the lower
edge of one side of the apron, stitching, as at

Fig. 8

b, to the top of the hem, then across the hem, as at *c*, and down the
other side to the bottom of the apron. Stitching in this way prevents the apron from tearing out at the ends, which, if left open, are
always in danger of being caught in something and thus being ripped
out, at least part way. With both thread ends on the wrong side
tie them in a secure knot, as at *d*.

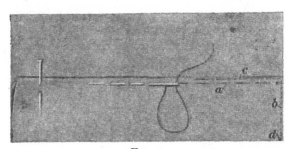

Fig. 9

14. Finishing and Applying the Pockets.—Fold the section of
material allowed for the pocket through the centre lengthwise, and
trim off the lower corners on a curved line. Then, with this shaped
pocket as a guide, cut a second one on exactly the same grain of the
material as the first, using for it the material cut away in section
b e f. First turn the straight edges across the top in a ¼-inch hem
and blanket-stitch over this hem, as at *a*, Fig. 10. Turn the other

edges in once and baste this turn, as at *b*. Then, with the apron on, decide on the position of the pockets by measuring down with the hand to a point that is convenient to reach. Remove and baste the pockets in position, as at *c*, keeping both exactly even.

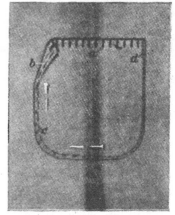

Next, stitch the pockets on, starting about 1 inch below the top of the pocket hem, as at *d*, stitching up to the top of the hem, and then turning the work and stitching down the same side, around the lower edge, and up to the opposite side to the top of the hem. Then turn the work again and stitch back along the side about 1 inch, as in the beginning, so as to provide a firm finish where there is a particular strain on the pocket. Tie these thread ends on the wrong side also.

FIG. 10

15. Making the Buttonhole.—If you have not had much previous experience with buttonholes, complete at least three, following

Fig. 39, *Essential Stitches and Seams*, before attempting to make the one in your apron belt. Then make this buttonhole in the right-hand end of the belt as perfect as possible, cutting it horizontally and using No. 50 cotton thread. Finally, sew on the button on the other end of the belt, as directed in Arts. 80 or 81, *Essential Stitches and Seams*.

Complete the apron by pressing it.

STEP-IN PANTIES

16. The pantie type of undergarment is widely accepted both because it is comfortable to wear and because it fits smoothly. The tailored type, illustrated in Fig. 11, can be quickly

FIG. 11

cut from a small amount of material and readily made up into an attractive garment.

17. Material Requirements and Measurements.—Any rayon or silk lingerie fabric is appropriate, while fine cottons, both plain and printed, may be chosen. Of any fabric, about 1¼ yards will be needed, but it is best to form the pattern first and then to determine the exact amount.

Three measurements must be taken, a snug waist, an easy hip 5, 6, or 7 inches below the waist line, depending on height, and the side length from the normal waist line to the desired point above the knee. If the waist measure is more than 9 inches smaller than the hip, use a proportionate measure and fit out the excess.

18. Forming the Pattern.—Provide a piece of paper 28 inches long and a little wider than the hip measure, and fold it through the lengthwise centre. Place this folded paper on your cutting table with the folded edge next to you, as in Fig. 12, and mark the corner at the lower right *a*. To the left of *a* on the fold, mark the following points : *b*, ½ inch from *a*, and *c*, 1 inch from *a*, for the

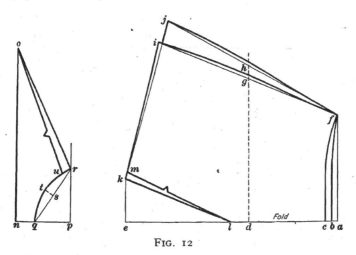

FIG. 12

back- and front-waist lines ; *d*, 5, 6, or 7 inches for the hip line ; and *e*, the length measure plus 1½ inches. On the cut edges of the paper locate *f* one-fourth the waist measure plus ½ inch from *a*. Join *b* and *f* and *c* and *f*, keeping the lines straight for 3 or 4 inches from *b* and *c* and then curving them gradually to *f*.

Straight up from *d*, draw a guide line one-fourth the hip measure plus 3 inches. On this line, mark *g* one-fourth the hip measure plus 1 inch, and *h*, 1 inch above *g*. With your ruler or yard-stick touching *f* and *g*, draw a line from *f* through *g* the pantie length and mark its end *i*. Draw a line the same length from *f* through *h* and mark its end *j*. To give a little more ease through the hips, locate points $\frac{1}{4}$ inch above *g* and *h* on the foundation hip line, and round out the side seam lines in long, easy curves that pass through these points and blend into straight lines at the ends, as shown.

To shape the lower section, draw a $3\frac{1}{4}$-inch guide line straight up from *e* and mark its end *k*. Join *k* and *i*, and *k* and *j*. On the fold, locate *l* to the right of *e* 7 inches for the short, 8 inches for the medium, and 9 inches for the tall person. Locate *m* $\frac{1}{2}$ inch above *k* on line *ki*. Join *k* and *l*, and *m* and *l*. To indicate the front, mark a notch in line *ml* 3 inches from *m*.

For the insert pattern, locate *n* on the fold 7 or 8 inches to the left of *e*. Draw a line straight up from *n* the length of *e* to *l* plus 3, 4, or 5 inches, depending on height, and mark its end *o*. To the right of *n* on the fold, locate *p* 4, $4\frac{1}{4}$, or $4\frac{1}{2}$ inches, depending on size. Draw a 6-inch guide line straight up from *p*. On the fold, locate *q* $1\frac{1}{4}$, $1\frac{1}{2}$, or $1\frac{3}{4}$ inches from *n*, depending on size. Locate *r*, 3, 4, or 5 inches above *p*, depending on height, and join *q* and *r* with a straight line. Midway between *q* and *r*, locate *s*, from it, to the left, draw a $\frac{3}{4}$-inch perpendicular guide line, and mark its end *t*. Join *q* and *r* with a curved line, passing through *t*. On the curved line, locate *u* $\frac{3}{4}$ inch from *r*. Join *u* and *o*, and *r* and *o* with straight lines, marking a notch in line *uo* 3 inches from *u* to indicate the front.

19. Cutting Out the Pattern.—With your tracing wheel, mark line *kj*. Then, through both thicknesses of the paper, cut from *b* to *f*, from *f* to *j* on the curved line, and from *l* to *k*. Open out the two thicknesses, cut on the fold, and mark the centre front on the upper piece and the centre back on the under piece, placing this marking on the inside of each piece. On the back section, cut from *k* to *j* on the traced line. On the front piece, cut from *c* to *f*, from *f* to *i* on the curved line, from *i* to *m*, and from *m* to *l*, cutting the notch to mark the front.

For the insert, cut through the double thickness from *q* to *r* through *t*, from *r* to *o*, and from *n* to *o*. Open out the paper and cut from *u* to *o*, cutting the notch to mark the front.

20. Cutting the Panties.—Lay the pattern pieces on your material as shown in Fig. 13, which is a layout for a 30-inch waist on

39-inch fabric, 1 yard of this width as well as 36-inch material being sufficient for this size. On a new fold of the right width, place the front and back as close together as possible and pin securely, but

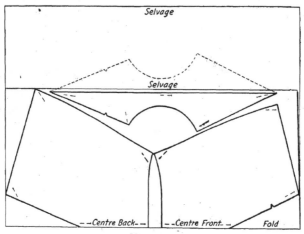

FIG. 13

make sure that the insert can be cut on a fold from the under thickness, the dotted lines representing the other half of the insert. Cut exactly on the outlines as the seams are allowed, and mark but do not cut the notch. Fold the remaining under piece to accommodate the insert, pin securely with the long straight edge on the fold, and cut exactly on the outlines, marking but not cutting the notch. At this time, cut the bias strips for finishing.

21. Cutting and Joining Bias Strips.—The first step in cutting bias strips is to obtain a true bias. As a beginner, it is well to start with a perfect corner ; therefore, select a piece of the material you intend to use for binding, having a selvage along one edge and the other edge cut exactly along a crosswise thread. When more experience has been gained, the true bias may be obtained without these precautions.

In order to have the ends of the bias strips along lengthwise edges, since these make the most satisfactory joinings, choose a section of fabric longer than it is wide and have it of a size that will make the strips at least 8 inches long. Shorter strips make it necessary to have too many joinings unless, of course, you are binding only a short section, when bias strips of merely the length of the section may be provided.

With your material prepared, place it on your cutting table with one crosswise edge next to you and the selvage to the left, as in Fig. 14, view (*a*), and, lifting the corner at the upper right, bring it toward you and fold it to the left over on the material so that the crosswise edge runs in the same direction as the lengthwise threads.

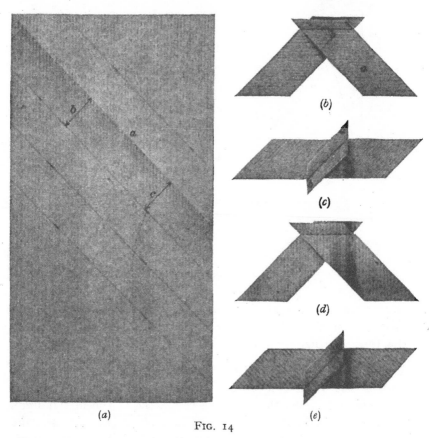

(*b*)

(*c*)

(*d*)

(*a*)   (*e*)

Fig. 14

In fact, the crosswise edge should exactly coincide with a lengthwise thread or, in this case, with the selvage of the material. Be very careful to make this turn accurate or your bias edge will not be true, so examine it for its entire length to make sure that it is perfect throughout. When you have made certain that the fold is correct, press it lightly to crease it, following the threads of the material with the iron so as not to stretch the bias edge. Then turn back the corner, when the crease will indicate a true bias line, as at *a*. If you started with a perfectly square corner, the distance from the corner along the crosswise edge to the crease will be the same as the distance from the corner along the lengthwise edge to the crease. Next, with the material smooth and flat, mark the width of the strips desired, measuring across the bias in several places at right angles to the crease, as at *b* and *c*, draw lines across the material through the points marked as guides for cutting as shown, and cut on these lines. In this case, for the bindings to finish the lower edges, as well as the facings for the top, make the strips 1 inch wide.

To join bias strips, trim the ends even, if necessary, preferably along a lengthwise thread, as previously suggested, place one strip *a*, Fig. 14, view (*b*), over the other at right angles, right sides together, and the points extending the width of the seam desired, from $\frac{3}{16}$ to $\frac{1}{4}$ inch. Baste along the straight edges from the exact point where the strips cross on one side to a similar point on the other. Stitch, exactly on a straight thread, then remove the bastings, when the seam will appear as at *b*. Next, press open. The finished seam on the wrong side is shown in view (*c*) with the bias edges even and continuous. Trim off the points *a* and *b* beyond the seam for an even edge.

In views (*d*) and (*e*), the appearance of a bias joining when crosswise threads meet is shown. Bring the perfectly cut edges together, as in view (*d*), the points extending for the seam width, baste and stitch as directed, and then press open, when the seam will appear as in view (*e*). Trim off the points to complete. Such joinings, of course, are frequently made, especially in plain weaves, but they should usually be avoided, particularly in the case of crosswise striped, or crosswise patterned material, for it is difficult to match stripes or pattern and therefore to produce a good effect.

22. Preparing the Panties for Fitting.—Turn the straight edges of the insert $\frac{3}{16}$ inch to the wrong side and baste without stretching, being careful to make a perfect point. Turn the point openings of the panties $\frac{3}{16}$ inch to the right side and baste, slashing the point to make the turn lie flat. Then, starting at the lower edge, pin the insert to the openings, front and back, as for a $\frac{3}{8}$-inch overlapped seam, the raw edges together at the bottom and the point extending up on the panties as far as it will go without any effect of stretching. Baste, then stitch close to the turns, right and wrong sides, and press. Baste up the side seams, raw edges to the right side in preparation for French seams, leaving the left one open 6 to 8 inches

at the top. Slip on the panties and pin together at the top. Fit
out any excess material in the side seams or in darts, 4 to 6 inches
long, each side of the centre front and back, making these ¼ inch
deep at the waist line and running them out to nothing at their ends.
Be sure to have the darts straight, and at even distances from the
centre lines.

23. Finishing the Side Seams and Opening.—Baste and stitch
on the wrong side any darts you used. Rebaste the side seams, if necessary, and complete the French seams, as in Fig. 33, *Essential Stitches
and Seams.* For the continuous placket finish, cut a straight facing

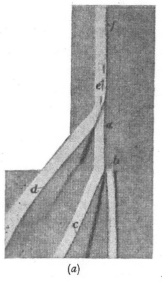

(a)   (b)

FIG. 15

strip 1½ inches wide and twice as long as the left-side opening. Trim
away the seam allowance, where it has been left open for the placket,
to within $\frac{3}{16}$ inch of the seam line. Baste, then stitch the facing to
the placket opening, as at *a*, Fig. 15, view (*a*), right sides together,
raw edges even, and the stitching in line with the seam stitching.
At the bottom of the opening, clip across the seam allowance where
the French seam ends, as at *b*, and continue the stitching to the top of
the other side, as at *c*. Press the stitching, then turn in the free
edge of the facing $\frac{3}{16}$ inch, as at *d*, baste it down, as at *e*, so that the
turned edge just covers the stitching, and whip to the stitching, as
at *f*.

24. Facing the Top.—With the placket extension turned against the front, as at *a*, and both sides of the opening exactly the same length, first baste, then stitch the bias facing to the upper edge of the panties, as at *b*, Fig. 15, view (*b*). Press this seam open as an aid to obtaining a flat sharp edge, then press it flat again. Turn in the ends, as at *c*, and the top edge, as at *d*, turn to the wrong side exactly on the seam, and baste close to the turn, as at *e*, and again along the inside edge, as at *f*. Whip, as at *g*, using very small stitches across the ends, as at *h*, or, if preferred, machine or slip-stitch. Overhand the cut edge of the French seam, as at *i*.

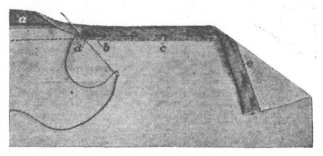

FIG. 16

25. Binding the Lower Edges.—Place the right side of your prepared binding to the right side of the panties, edges even, and baste, beginning about 1 inch from the end of the bias and continuing around the leg opening to within 1 inch of the beginning of the binding, this space being left so that the two ends may be joined. Cut the bias along straight threads so that the ends meet in a ¼-inch seam and the bias exactly fits the edge, join the ends exactly as you made the other joinings, press open the seam, and then complete the basting of the binding to the garment. Replace the basting with stitching ¼ inch from the edge, turn under the free edge ¼ inch, as at *a*, Fig. 16, bring this edge just to the first stitching, as at *b*, and baste in place, as at *c*. Then whip, as at *d*, taking the stitches through the machine stitching instead of through the material so that none will appear on the right side, as at *e*.

Because the application of bias for edge finishes is so important in dressmaking, it is well always to keep in mind certain points in connection with it. One of these is to start to apply the bias on the garment where the joining will be inconspicuous, for one of the niceties of fine sewing is to conceal the utilitarian seam.

In this case, just back of the side seam will be a good place to make the joining, in order to avoid excess seamings in the front section.

Another important point to remember is that any tendency to looseness in the bias will cause an unattractive, uneven appearance in the finished effect. So try to acquire, through practice, the right tension at which to hold the bias when you are basting it in place. On comparatively straight edges, as in the case of the panties, hold the bias just easy, neither tight nor loose. But on a rounded or bias edge, hold the binding strip rather taut so that this edge will not ripple when the binding is completed.

26. Finishing the Panties.—Press the panties. Then mark for horizontal buttonholes in the left-side front and make them, as directed in Arts. 69 to 77, inclusive, *Essential Stitches and Seams*, to accommodate ⅜-inch buttons. Sew the buttons to the back as directed in either Art. 80 or 81, *Essential Stitches and Seams*. If preferred, a hook and eye may be used at the waist band and snap fasteners on the opening.

BODICE SLIP

27. A very important item in the wardrobe is the costume slip, the style illustrated in Fig. 17 fulfilling practically every requirement of this type of undergarment. Simple in its every phase of making, individual because it is cut to measure, and practical because it relies on good lines and sensible construction for its appeal, it should, if properly developed through every step of the clear directions that follow, fit you with the same accuracy and fashionable chic as the dress you wear over it.

FIG. 17

The bodice top of the slip is smooth and sleek, and, being joined at the waist line to the gently flared skirt section, permits of a trim waist line, always a desirable feature in such a garment. As shown in the small view, the skirt section may be made up in evening length and finished as a petticoat. Or, in this length, it may be sewed to the bodice top to make a full-length slip.

28. Material Requirements and Measurements.—If possible, a silk or rayon fabric should be selected for a slip because of its smoothness and clinging qualities. The various crepe weaves are most frequently used, but satin and taffeta also are very satisfactory, particularly for more dressy wear. If a cotton slip is wanted, longcloth and nainsook are suitable. The regulation lingerie colours, flesh, tea rose, and white, are recommended for this slip, as well as beige, grey, or the colour of any particular dress. Of any fabric, the person of average height will require about $2\frac{1}{4}$ yards, the shorter figure less, and the taller figure, more. But, for the greatest accuracy, it is best to form the pattern first and then determine by actual measurement the amount required.

Three measurements are needed, the bust, the hip, both taken snugly, and the skirt length, taken from the waist line at about the location of the under-arm seam down over the hip to the usual slip length, that is, about 1 inch shorter than your dresses.

29. Forming the Pattern.—For this slip, the bodice back and the skirt front are blocked out, and from these original patterns the bodice front and the skirt back are later formed by the introduction of darts and, in the case of the bodice front, some additional shaping of a simple nature. Because of this, the preparation of the cutting guide is readily done, provided, of course, each step in the process is accurately followed.

For the pattern, you will need a section of paper as long as a generous slip length and about 40 inches wide. Fold this accurately through the lengthwise centre and place it on your cutting table with the long open edges next to you.

First, as in Fig. 18, view (a), mark the corner at the lower right a. Measure up from a a distance equal to one-fourth the bust measure plus $\frac{3}{4}$ inch and mark b. From b, measure to the left the under-arm length, $7\frac{1}{2}$ inches for the short, $8\frac{1}{2}$ inches for the medium, and $9\frac{1}{2}$ inches for the tall figure, draw a line this distance parallel to the edge of the paper, and mark its end c. From a, along the edge of the paper, measure the same distance as *c* is from *b*, mark *d*, and connect *c* and *d* with a line.

To shape this section, measure to the left of *b* 1 inch and mark *e*, measure toward you from *c* 1 inch and mark *f*, and measure to the right of *d* ½ inch and mark *g*. Draw a line straight up from *g* and mark *h*, having this line 3 inches for the slender, 3½ inches for the

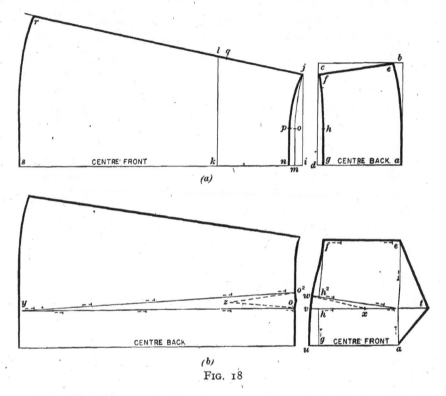

Fig. 18

medium, and 4 inches for the stout figure. Join *e* and *f* with a straight line, and draw slightly curved lines from *e* to line *ab* and from *f* to *h*, as indicated.

To form the foundation skirt pattern, measure to the left of *d* a few inches and place point *i*. Straight up from *i*, locate point *j* the same distance from *i* that *f* is from *d*. To the left of *i*, measure 7½ inches for the short, 8½ inches for the medium, and 9½ inches for the tall figure and locate point *k*. Then, straight up from *k*, measure one-fourth the hip measure plus 1 inch, draw a guide line this length, and mark its end *l*. With your yardstick, join *j* and *l* and continue the line to approximately the skirt length of your slip.

To shape the waist line of the skirt, measure to the left of i ¾ inch and mark m; then beyond m, measure ½ inch and mark n. Draw a straight line up from both m and n, each 3 inches long for the slender figure, 3½ inches for the medium-size figure, and 4 inches for the stout figure, and mark them o and p, respectively. Join j and o and j and p with curved lines, as indicated. The upper line moj is for the back, and the lower one npj for the front waist line.

To obtain the lower edge line, first mark point q the same distance from j that k is from m; then measure to the left of q the side skirt length minus the distance from q to j and mark r. Then, to the left of k, measure the same distance and mark point s. Join s to r with a line straight out from s for a distance of 5 or 6 inches, and then curved to r.

Now trace the outline of these two sections through to the under thickness of paper, tracing from a to e to f and to g for the bodice section, and from m to j through o, to r through q and l, and from r to s. Mark the location of point o through to under section also. Cut on the traced lines, the under skirt portion to be used for the back, the upper one to be cut from n to j through p to provide for the deeper front curve.

To form the upper front pattern, as in view (b), draw a straight line to the right from h to within ¼ inch of the top edge, keeping it parallel to the centre front, and cut on this line. Then pin the centre-front line along the straight edge of a section of paper slightly wider than the back section and about 5 inches longer, spread the slash to provide a space of 1 inch at its lower edge, and pin, as shown. Mark the opposite edge of the dart opening h^2.

To shape the upper edge, draw a guide line straight up from the top in line with the slash a distance of 3 inches and mark its end t. Draw a line from a to t and another from t to e to provide the pointed shaping.

To shape the waist-line edge, mark point u 1 inch to the left of g, extend the dart slash edges with straight lines, one ¾ inch to the left of h, marking its end v, and the other ¾ inch to the left of h^2, making its end w. Draw the new waist line from u to f through v and w, as shown.

For the dart, measure up from v a distance of 5½ inches, mark x, and draw a line from w to x. The stitching lines for the dart will be vx and wx.

Cut this section from a to t to e to f, but, before cutting across the lower edge line, crease your pattern along the dart line vx, bring the crease over to the other dart edge wx, and pin. Then cut from u to f through v, thus forming a lower edge line that will be correct when the garment is cut and the dart stitched and pressed.

For the back-skirt section, measure in $3\frac{1}{2}$ inches from the centre back at the lower skirt edge and mark y. Draw a line from o to within $\frac{1}{4}$ inch of y and slash on this line. Place a section of paper underneath extending an inch or two above the waist line, spread the slash $1\frac{1}{4}$ inches at the waist line, graduating it to nothing toward the lower edge, and pin, as shown. Mark the opposite end of the dart opening at the waist line o^2.

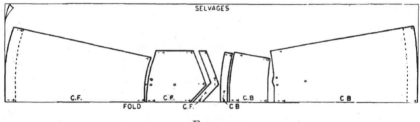

FIG. 19

Next, locate a point in the centre of the dart space about $6\frac{1}{2}$ inches from the waist-line edge and mark it z. Then, for the dart, draw lines from point z to the edges of the opening at the waist line, o and o^2. Fold in the dart by creasing on the line oz and bring it to o^2z, then trim off the excess length of the paper inset, following the original waist-line edge. When the dart is opened out again, it will appear with a slight upward shaping, as indicated.

To provide the patterns for the facings that finish the upper edge of the slip, pin the front and back to paper, centre front and centre back along straight edges. Cut around the top lines, and down the side seams for a distance of about 3 inches. Then, with your ruler or gauge, measure at intervals from the top edges downward a distance of $2\frac{1}{2}$ inches and place points. Join these points to form a continuous line and trace on the lines just drawn. Remove the bodice sections and cut on the traced lines underneath, thus forming the facing patterns. Next, so that the location of the darts may be transferred to your material, clip small openings in the patterns, one at the tip of each of the darts and one on each of the lines that mark the outside edges of the darts, placing these a seam's width inside the cutting line.

30. Cutting and Marking the Slip.—With the material folded through the lengthwise centre, place it on your cutting table with the fold nearest you. Follow the layout given in Fig. 19 for the arrangement of the various pattern sections, placing the centre front and centre back in each case along the fold. The illustration shows new pattern sections cut with 2-inch hem allowances. Pin all parts accurately in place, being sure to keep the centres exactly along the folds, as indicated. Now cut carefully around the pattern outlines allowing for a 2-inch hem at the lower skirt edges, if you have not cut a new pattern.

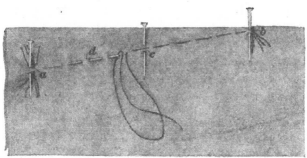

FIG. 20

Cut straight strips for the shoulder straps from one thickness of the remaining material. Trim away the selvage for a distance of about 1 yard, and provide a strip about 1¼ inches wide and 1 yard long, first drawing a thread to insure straight edges.

Before removing the pattern, mark the front-bodice and back-skirt darts, following the instruction given in Art. 47 and illustrated in view (b), Fig. 15, *Essential Stitches and Seams*. Remove the pattern, next draw the two thicknesses of material carefully apart, and clip the mark-stitching threads, when they will appear as at c and d, view (c), Fig. 15.

31. Preparing the Slip for Fitting.—The first step is basting the darts. In preparation for this, pin them, being guided by the mark-stitches. Bring together those which indicate the dart width at its wide end, and run a pin through both thicknesses of material exactly in the mark-stitches, as at a, Fig. 20, this section. Place a second pin through the mark-stitch that indicates the inside end of the dart, as at b, and a third one between these two, as at c. Now baste along the line of pins, as at d. With the basting of all four darts completed, replace the basting with stitching and tie the threads at the ends carefully. Press thoroughly, turning both bodice and skirt darts away from the centre lines.

Next, prepare the waist-line joinings for the overlapped seam and complete the basting of them as directed in Art. 67 *Essential Stitches and Seams*. In this case, the skirt sections lap over the bodice. Pin, then baste the under-arm seams, matching the waist-line joinings and the upper edges of the slip perfectly and turning the seam allowance to the right side for finishing as a French seam later on.

Next, stitch and turn the shoulder straps as directed for the bib strap in Art. 11 of this section, using a knitting needle or a crochet hook for turning if a pencil is too thick. Cut off the stitched end, and then press the straps with the seam in the centre. Mark two points at the top of the slip, each about 3½ inches from the centre-back point. Pin one end of each of the shoulder straps here and the other end at the tip of the front points, having the length of the straps about 16 to 18 inches.

32. **Fitting the Slip.**—Put the slip on over the usual under-garments, adjust the shoulder straps, changing their position in the back or their length if necessary, and observe the bust and hip sections and the location of the waist-line joining. If the latter seems low, raise it entirely around the figure or at a particular section. If the slip seems loose, fit it for a smooth but easy effect, making the alteration entirely on the front or the back or dividing it evenly between the two. Remove the slip, mark any new seam lines with basting-stitches in contrasting thread through only a single thickness of material, mark the length and position of the shoulder straps, and rebaste the waist-line seam, if necessary. Remove all pins.

33. **Finishing the Waist Line and Top.**—Clip the basting of the under-arm seam at the waist line and rip open this seam to the top. Then stitch the waist-line joining, as at *f*, Fig. 36, *Essential Stitches and Seams*.

Next, prepare to apply the facing to the top edge. As shown in Fig. 21, this section, first pin the facings in place with their right sides to the right side of the garment, as at *a*, replace the pins with basting, as at *b*, remove the pins, and then stitch, as at *c*. Remove the bastings and then clip the seam allowance in preparation for turning the facing to the wrong side so that this turn may be properly made ; that is, trim away the points, as at *d*, cut down to the stitching, but not through it, at the centre front, as at *e*, and cut in the width of the seam allowance, as at *f*, and at the corresponding point

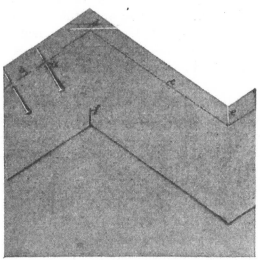

FIG. 21

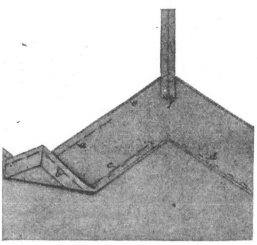

FIG. 22

on the other side. It is always a help, when turning a facing, to have the seam pressed, so, with the tip of a hot iron, press open as much as possible of the seam that joins the facing to the garment.

Next, back and front, turn the facing to the wrong side, and, keeping the seam exactly on the edge, baste close to the turn, as at *a*, Fig. 22. Next, turn back the free edge a seam's width and baste, as at *b*, first pin and then baste this edge flat to the garment, as at *c*, and stitch the facing in place, as at *d*. Replace the shoulder straps, back and front, in their proper position by pinning and basting. From the right side, stitch close to the top edge, as at *e*, catching in the shoulder straps with this stitch, as shown. Treat the back similarly.

Now, trim off the ends of the shoulder straps to within about ¾ inch of the stitching, turn in the raw edges and whip them down to the facing, as at *f*. Take care not to have any of these stitches go through to the right side. Then, remove all bastings and press.

34. Finishing Slip.—Replace the under-arm bastings that have been removed, and join the under arms with French seams, as directed in Art. 64, *Essential Stitches and Seams*. Press thoroughly. Then put on the slip in readiness for marking the lower edge. If a skirt marker or gauge is on hand, use it because of its accuracy and time-saving qualities. If not, a yardstick makes a very satisfactory substitute.

When there is some one else to do the work for you, decide on the distance from the floor which you wish the slip to be, usually 1 to 1½ inches shorter than your dresses; then have the person helping you locate this point on the yardstick. Have her hold it in a steady upright position just touching the skirt and place pins entirely around the skirt in line with the point located on the yardstick. To insure accuracy, stand firmly on both feet, and, when the pins are being placed, turn slowly around. While the slip is still on, the hem should be turned up accurately on the marked line.

If it is necessary for you to mark the length unaided, stand a yardstick upright on the floor with one end touching your figure, and place marks or pins on the skirt at the top of the stick, or at your hip line, moving the stick around the figure. With the slip still on the figure, turn up the lower front edge to decide on the length. Remove, measure down the same distance from each mark, and place pins. With the length marked, finish the hem as shown in Fig. 29, *Essential Stitches and Seams*. Then, overcast the raw edges of the waist-line seam.

OVERBLOUSE

35. To complete a suit, or to wear with a separate skirt, a blouse, such as the one illustrated in Fig. 23, will be found both practical and attractive. Its chic collar and bow, youthful short sleeves, and trimly fitted hip section are noteworthy points, while its ease of cutting and making give it further appeal. However, it is suitable for figures only up to 40-inch bust measure.

36. Material Requirements and Measurements.—Any medium-weight silk like flat crêpe, satin, or taffeta, plain or printed, or cottons that are not transparent, are appropriate materials, only $1\frac{5}{8}$ yards being needed for practically any figure for which the design is suitable. If the hip size is less than 36 inches, 36-inch fabric may be used, but for larger sizes, 39-inch material should be used. Also, provide a small belt buckle.

FIG. 23

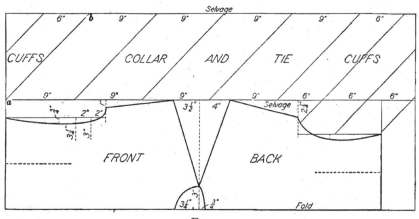

FIG. 24

Take four measurements as follows, taking all easily; one from the blouse length in front, up over the shoulder, to a corresponding point in back; your bust measure; your hip measure; and your upper arm at its fullest part.

37. Cutting the Blouse.—Because of its simplicity, you may locate the various points directly on your material. First trim away a 4-inch strip across the width for the belt; then make a fold 12½ inches from one selvage, if your hip measure is less than 36 inches, or 14 inches if it is 36 inches or more. With the fold nearest you, as in Fig. 24, indicate a point on the fold the front-to-back measurement plus 4 inches from the left end and draw a line to the selvage. Mark the exact lengthwise centre of this section on the fold, mark a point ¾ inch to the right of the centre, from it draw a guide line to the selvage, and indicate on it a point 3 inches from the fold. On the fold, mark a point ¼ inch to the right of the guide line, and one 3¼ inches to the left, and join to the 3-inch point on the guide line with curved lines for the neck line, as shown.

On the selvage, mark a point 3¼ inches to the left of the guide line, and join this to the neck curve for the front-shoulder line. To the left again, mark a point one-half the arm measure plus 2 inches from the end of the shoulder line, and from it draw a 3-inch guide line toward the fold. On this, mark a point 1 inch from the selvage and connect it by means of a straight line with the end of the shoulder line for the lower sleeve edge.

From the lower left corner, mark a point on the raw edges one-fourth the hip measure plus 2 inches, and from it draw a line parallel to the selvage to intersect the under-arm guide line. Mark a point 2 inches below the intersection, and another 2 inches below the first, and from these points mark 3- to 4½-inch darts, as shown, the lower one ¼ inch longer then the upper. To shape the under arm, draw a ¾-inch guide line toward the fold about 7 inches from the raw edges and draw a curved under-arm line from the raw edges, passing through the end of this line and extending to the lower edge of the sleeve, as shown.

On the selvage, mark a point 4 inches to the right of the centre guide line and connect this with the neck edge for the back-shoulder line. To the right again, mark a point one-half the arm measure plus 2 inches from the end of the shoulder line, and draw a 5-inch guide line toward the fold. On this, mark a point 2¼ inches from the selvage and connect it with the end of the shoulder line for the sleeve edge. From the lower right corner of the back, mark a point on the lower edge one-fourth the hip measure, and from it draw a line to intersect the under-arm guide line. Shape the back under-arm line as you did the front. Halfway between the fold and the under-arm line, on the lower-edges, draw 9-inch guide lines for the darts that fit the waist line.

Cut the neck line, then the front shoulder, the sleeve edge, and the curved under-arm line, rounding the corner slightly. Cut the back section in a similar manner.

From the section remaining, mark and then cut bias strips for the collar and tie and the cuffs. Starting at the left, turn down the upper corner so that the crosswise cut edge lies directly in line with the lengthwise threads, and thus form a true bias *ab*. Press lightly on the fold, and lay the corner back. From both points *a* and *b*, measure 9 inches to your right, and join these two points with a light pencil line, marking off four such strips. From the corner sections, mark off 6-inch strips, as shown, for the cuffs.

38. Making and Fitting the Blouse.—Mark-stitch the under-arm and hip darts. Baste the under-arm darts, as in Fig. 20, from nothing at the inside end to a width at the edge that will make the front under arm the same length as the back one. Baste the hip darts from nothing 1½ inches from the edge to about ½ inch at the waist line, and then out to nothing at the top. Baste the under-arm and shoulder seams. Slash the centre-front line from the neck edge for about 5 inches and bind with a ¾-inch bias, as in Fig. 16. Join the bias sections for the collar and tie, joining the selvages where ever possible, and for the cuffs, as in Fig. 14, view (*b*). Press each seam thoroughly and trim off the points as directed.

First pin, and then baste, one long edge of the collar to the blouse, its centre to the centre back point of the neck line. Now, fold the tie ends, right side in, so that their long raw edges exactly meet, then pin, baste, and stitch them, also stitching across the ends following a straight thread of the material. Remove the bastings, tie the thread ends, trim away any excess seam allowance at the ends, and turn right side out. Baste along the seam, keeping the seam exactly on the edge.

Turn and baste a 1½-inch hem around the lower edge of the blouse. Stitch, turn, and press the belt as for straps in Art. 11. Slip the blouse on, bow the tie becomingly, and pin the belt in place. If necessary, deepen or let out the hip darts under the under-arm seams. Mark the position of the belt.

39. Finishing the Blouse.—Stitch the darts, the under-arm seams, clipping them at their curves, and the shoulder seams. Stitch the collar to the neck line, turn in the free edge $\frac{1}{4}$ inch, and whip to the stitching as for bias binding, Fig. 16. Apply the cuffs like the collar but have the whipped edge to the right side. Slip-stitch the hem. Sew the buckle to one end of the belt and tack the belt at the under-arm seams. Turn back the collar to half its width, and the cuffs full width, and tack them in place also. Press thoroughly.

VARIETY BLOUSE

40. When a blouse of a more formal character is wanted, the surplice type shown in Fig. 25 may well be selected. Possess-ing charm and chic, its rippled shoulder extension and smartly tied belt are attractive fea-tures. As a suit blouse, it is very youthful in effect, for dinner and informal evening occasions, especially when combined with a floor length skirt, it is suited to the digni-fied wearer as well.

FIG. 25

41. Material Requirements. Because of its cut and design features, this blouse will look its best when developed of a crisp material and when worn by the slender or medium size person, since those having a bust measure larger than 40 inches will find such a style unbecoming.

Taffeta, moire, metallic, organdie, plain or embroidered, and even gingham are waves that will look well when cut over these lines, although one of the softer textures may be used if it is not objection-able to have the shoulder pleats fall in soft folds rather than stand out pertly as in Fig. 25.

Of the material selected, from $1\frac{1}{8}$ to $1\frac{1}{4}$ yards will be needed, the actual amount to be determined after the pattern has been made.

42. Taking Measurements.—To form the pattern, you will need four measurements, the bust, the waist, the blouse length or over-the-shoulder measure, and the girth of the upper arm. Measure around the bust at its fullest part easily, that is, with the tape measure easy but not loose, measure around the waist closely, and measure around the fullest part of the arm, taking this closely too. For the over-the-shoulder measure, place one end of the tape at the back waist line, and then run it up over the shoulder close to the neck and down to the front waist line. This measure is used to determine the length of the pattern and is much better when generous than scanty, for a blouse can be shortened after being cut but it is practically impossible to lengthen it.

43. Forming the Pattern.—Since it is necessary first to make a pattern for the blouse, provide a section of paper as long as the over-the-shoulder measure plus 2 or 3 inches and about 14 to 16 inches wide. With one long edge of the paper toward you, as in Fig. 26, view (a) mark point a in the corner at the lower right, and then measure to the left from a the over-the-shoulder measure and place point b. Next, from point a, measure straight up a distance equal to one-fourth the bust measure plus $2\frac{1}{2}$ inches and mark c. Draw a line the same length straight up from b, calling its end d, and connect points c and d to form a rectangle.

For the neck line and shoulder shaping, first locate point e in the centre of the line ab, as shown, and draw a line straight up to line cd and mark its end f. On this line, locate point g $2\frac{1}{2}$ inches from e; to the right, locate h $\frac{1}{2}$ inch from e, and to the left, locate i 3 inches from e. Connect points h and g and i and g, as shown, for the back and front neck-line curves. Next, locate point j 2 inches to the right and k 2 inches to the left of point f. Connect points j and g and k and g for the shoulder lines.

For the arm openings, locate point l one-half the arm-girth measure plus $3\frac{1}{2}$ inches to the right of j and point m one-half the arm-girth measure plus 2 inches to the left of k. From these points, draw 4-inch guide lines straight toward you, as indicated. On the guide line from point l, locate n 1 inch from l. Connect j and n. In the centre of the space mk, draw a $\frac{3}{4}$-inch guide line perpendicular to it, and draw the front armhole line by connecting points m and k with a shallow curved line passing through the end of the guide line, as shown.

Next, plan and place the back waist line and under-arm lines. From point a, measure toward c a distance equal to one-fourth the

waist measure plus 2 inches and mark *o*. To the left of *o* and perpendicular to *ac*, draw a guide line to meet the guide line from *l*.
Then draw a curve, as shown, across the angle formed by the meeting of the two lines. Next, locate a point ½ inch from *o* toward *a*
and mark it *p*. Join point *p* to the end of the curved under-arm
section to complete the back under-arm line.

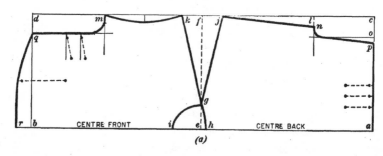

(a)

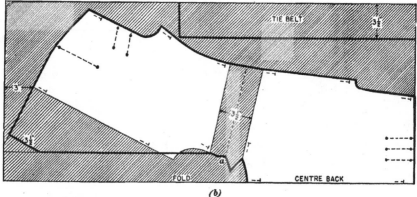

(b)

FIG. 26

For the front waist line and under-arm lines, first measure from *b*
toward *d* a distance equal to one-fourth the waist measure plus 2
inches and mark *q*. Draw a line to the right of *q* and perpendicular
to *bd* to meet the guide line from *m* and draw a shallow curve across
the angle formed, as indicated, first marking points 1 inch from the
corner as guides for the beginning and end of the curved line.

Mark guide lines for the under-arm darts. For the figure of
average size, mark the first about 3½ inches above the waist line and
the second 1½ inches from the first, and make them perpendicular to
the under arm and about 2¼ inches long. Variation in their position,
is caused by the variable length of the under arm, but about the

centre of the under-arm space will usually be found satisfactory. Then locate points $\frac{1}{2}$ inch to the right of their inside ends, and join these points to the under-arm line at the dart location, thus forming slanting dart lines, as shown.

To provide the additional length needed across the front, locate point r $1\frac{1}{2}$ inches to the left of b and join r to q with a line that extends straight from r for a distance of 3 to 4 inches and then curves upward to q, as indicated.

For the necessary fitting darts that extend upward from the back waist line, mark these guide lines each about 3 inches long, the first 2 inches from the centre back, the others spaced 1 inch apart. Also, in about the centre of the front section, draw in a guide line for a dart extending straight up from the lower edge a distance of about 5 inches. As in the case of the front under-arm darts, these fitting darts may be slightly shorter, while those in the back may be closer to the centre back when the figure is small.

44. Cutting the Pattern.—Starting at a, cut to p, to n on the curve, then from n to j to g and to h along the neck curve. Start again at i and cut to g to k and to m through the curve. Now, cut from m through the under-arm curve and then straight down to q and from q to r along the new waist line. Clip perforations at the location of the darts, one at the end of each dart and one the width of the seam allowance, that is, $\frac{3}{8}$ inch, inside the pattern edge. It will be a simple matter to transfer the location of the darts to your material through these perforations.

45. Determining the Yardage.—At this time, if you have not already purchased your material, you may determine the exact amount needed by arranging the pattern pieces as shown in view (b). Place the back section so that the centre-back line is straight and then place the front with its shoulder line parallel to the back shoulder line and separated from it $3\frac{1}{2}$ inches at every point. For the yardage needed, add about 3 inches to the space covered by the pattern.

46. Cutting Out the Blouse.—Leave your material in its original lengthwise fold, or fold it accurately through the lengthwise centre if it is not already folded, and place it on your table with the folded edge nearest you, as shown. At the right end, place the back section with its centre-back line along the fold and pin. Now, with tailor's chalk and a ruler, mark a guide line $3\frac{1}{2}$ inches from the back shoulder line, and place the shoulder line of the front pattern along the line just drawn, having its outside end extend about $\frac{1}{2}$ inch beyond the outside end of the back, as indicated. Pin in this position.

Then, with tailor's chalk and your yard-stick, mark a line to the left from the inside end of the front-shoulder line to the end of the material, having this parallel to the folded edge, as shown. Extend the lower blouse edge to form the surplice lap, finishing off the end with a straight line about $3\frac{1}{2}$ inches long and parallel to the original front edge of the blouse pattern, as shown.

Start to cut at the waist line of the back under-arm seam, continue along the back armhole and across the open space in a straight line to the front armhole opening, and then along this and the under-arm to the front waist line. Then, follow the pattern outline across the lower front edge to the end of the surplice lap and along the marked lines to the tip of the front shoulder line. Before cutting across the open space between front and back, mark the additional lines for the pleats, as indicated, one line along the back pattern edge and the other in the centre of the space, the front pattern edge already being marked. Fold your material to form an inverted pleat, bringing the fold along the front shoulder to the centre space and pinning, and doing the same with the back fold. With the material folded, cut across the fold at the neck line and then to the centre back. When the material at the shoulder is opened out, it will appear as at *a*.

From the section remaining along the selvages, cut two strips for the tie belt, as indicated, making these about $3\frac{1}{2}$ inches wide, the average length being about 28 inches. From the pieces that remain, cut bias strips for the facings that finish the edges, making these about 1 inch wide. However, if you prefer, you may purchase ready-cut and folded bias binding in a colour and texture to harmonize with your blouse material.

47. Marking and Preparing for Fitting.—Before removing the pattern sections from the material, place a row of mark stitches along each of the shoulder lines, as well as along the line that indicates the centre of the space for pleating. Then mark-stitch through the perforations that indicate the position of the darts, following either Art. 46 or Art. 47, *Essential Stitches and Seams*. Unpin the pattern pieces, draw the mark-stitches apart carefully, and clip the threads in the centre.

Fold the shoulder pleats on the marked lines and bring them to the centre line to form an inverted pleat, first pinning and then basting in position. Then pin and baste the darts, making the under-arm darts and the one each side of the centre front ½ inch deep and those in the back ¼ inch deep at their outside ends, and tapering all the darts to nothing at their inside ends.

48. Some of the stitching may be done next. Starting at the neck edge, stitch along one fold of the shoulder pleat for a distance of 3 inches, if the figure is small, or 3½ inches for the medium or larger type ; then turn the material and continue the stitching along the other fold. Repeat for the other shoulder pleat. Then stitch the darts along the basted lines. Also, baste and stitch the tie ends to the ends of the surplice. Baste the under-arm seams next, leaving a 1½ inch space in the right under-arm 1 inch above the lower edge to provide a slit through which the tie belt may be run.

49. Fitting and Finishing the Blouse.—At this time, slip the blouse on to check its appearance. Because it has been cut to measure and because it is adjustable, it is not likely that any changes will be necessary. But, if you feel that any are required, make them at this time, such as, for instance, a small dart-like tuck on each side of the back neck line for better fitting at this place, or, perhaps the shortening of the blouse for becomingness. Remove the blouse, stitch the under-arm seams, leaving the unbasted space in the right one free, tie all thread ends securely, and press the seams and darts. To strengthen the under-arm opening, stitch entirely around it close to the turned edge.

Stitch the bias strips together now, as directed in Art. 21, press all the seams open carefully, and prepare to apply the bias facings. Attach the facings to the neck line and surplice, the armhole openings, and the lower edge of the blouse, basting and stitching them in place as directed for binding in Art. 25. The facings may also be continued around the edges of the tie belts, if desired, although a very narrow slip-stitched hem makes a satisfactory finish for them. After the first stitching has been completed, press open the seam, bring the facing back to the wrong side, keeping the seam exactly in the turn, and baste close to the edge. Turn in the free edge from to $\frac{3}{16}$ inch, hold the turn with small running-stitches, baste this turn flat to the garment, and complete with slip-stitching, as directed in Art. 59, *Essential Stitches and Seams*. If the tie belts have not been faced, turn and baste a narrow hem around them and complete with slip-stitching. Remove all bastings and press the blouse thoroughly, particularly around the edges.

FIG. 27

SHOULDER-RUFFLE NIGHTGOWN

50. The nightgown shown in Fig. 27 combines a very attractive appearance with simplicity of cutting and ease of making. Its ruffled shoulder fulness, provided in cutting, is youthful and appealing, its slightly fitted effect retains all the comfortable easy lines that such a garment should have, and its edge finish of self- or contrasting binding is simple and in the best of taste.

51. Material Requirements.— Nainsook and longcloth are desirable cotton materials for this garment, also special lingerie materials, both plain and figured, obtainable in silk, satin and rayon.

To determine the amount of material needed, measure the figure in front from shoulder to floor, multiply by two, and add 6 inches to provide the extra length needed for cutting the shoulder ruffle. The result will usually be about $3\frac{5}{8}$ yards for the person of average height. At this time, take the bust and hip measures.

For the pattern, provide a piece of plain paper twice the length of the nightgown and from 18 to 20 inches wide, depending on the width of your material. If necessary, the required size may be obtained by pasting or sewing together several sections.

52. Forming the Pattern.—Fold the paper through the crosswise centre and place it on your table with the fold at the right, as shown in Fig. 28. Mark *a* at the lower right corner, and *b* 1 inch to the left of *a* along the centre-front and back lines. To the left of *b*, locate *c* ¾ inch and *d*, 3¼ inches.

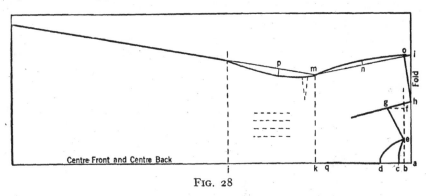

FIG. 28

Now, from *b*, draw out at right angles to the centre lines a dotted line 8 to 10 inches long and on it locate *e* from *b*, 2½ inches for the small, 3 inches for the medium, and 3¼ inches for the large figure. To make the back neck-line curve, connect *c* and *e* as shown, drawing the line straight out from *c* for about 1 inch and then curving to *e*, as indicated. Connect *d* and *e* for the front neck-line curve, drawing the line straight from *d* for about ½ inch and then curving it to *e*, as shown.

. To determine the shoulder seam, measure from *e* along the dotted lines 3 inches for the small, 4 inches for the medium, and 5 inches for the large figure, and mark *f*. To the left of *f* and at right angles to t, draw a 2-inch dotted line and mark its end *g*. Connect *g* and *e* for the shoulder line.

On the crosswise fold, locate *h* from *a*, 7 inches for the small, 8 nches for the medium, and 9 inches for the large figure, and locate *i* rom *h*, 5 inches for the small, 6 inches for the medium, and 7 inches or the large figure. Connect *h* and *g* with a straight line, continuing it 4½ to 5 inches beyond *g*, as shown.

Mark point *j* for the hip line 22 inches from *b* for the short, 24 inches or the medium, and 26 inches for the tall figure. Locate *k* midway etween *j* and *b* for the bust line. Draw up from *j*, at right angles) the centre lines, a dotted line equal to one-fourth the hip measure lus 3 inches and mark *l*. From *k*, draw a similar dotted line one-. .

fourth the bust measure plus 2 inches and mark *m*. With the edge of your yardstick touching points *l* and *m*, draw a line from *m* through *l* to the crosswise cut edges of the paper.

Connect *m* and *i* and locate *n* midway between them. From *n*, draw a $\frac{1}{2}$-inch line at right angles to line *mi*, and draw a curved line from *m* to *i* through the end of this line. Locate *o*, 1 inch from *i* on the curved line, and connect *h* and *o*.

To shape the under-arm, mark *p* on the under-arm line 4 inches to the left of *m* for the small, 5 inches for the medium, and 6 inches for the tall figure. Draw a 1-inch line toward you at right angles to *p*,

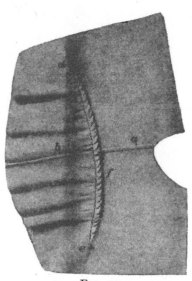

and then draw in a new curved under-arm line from *m* to *l* through the end of this line. Mark *q* on the centre-front line 6 to 7 inches from *d* for the centre-front slash.

About 2 inches below *m*, locate the under-arm dart, making this 3 inches long and 1 inch deep for the small, 1$\frac{1}{2}$ inches for the medium, and 2 inches for the large figure, and tapering it to nothing. Locate the waist-line tucks midway between the bust and hip lines, 5 inches long and 1 inch apart, the first 3 inches from the centre line.

FIG. 29

53. Cutting Out the Pattern.— Mark the waist-line tucks through to the back section with your tracing wheel. Then, cut from *c* to *e* to *g* and from *g* to the end of the dart slash. Next, cut to *h* and from *h* to *o* to *m* through the curved line, and from *m* to *l*, also through the curved line, to the lower edge. Separate the two sections, and cut from *d* to *e* for the front neck line.

54. Cutting Out the Nightgown.—Fold your material through the lengthwise centre, and place the two pattern pieces on it, their centre lines exactly on the folds. Pin carefully and generously, then cut accurately around all edges. Cut the centre-front slash and the slash for the shoulder-line fulness. From the remaining material cut a strip 2$\frac{1}{2}$ inches wide and as long as needed for the belt, piecing if necessary. Also, if self-fabric bias is being used for binding, cut the needed amount as directed in Art. 21. Mark-stitch the front under-arm darts and the waist-line tucks, as in Art. 47, *Essential Stitches and Seams*, using three tailor's tacks to each one, but first making small holes in the pattern so that the mark-stitches need not be taken through the paper. Clip the loops and remove the pattern.

55. Making the Nightgown.—With the tailor's tacks cut between the two thicknesses, pin, baste, and stitch the under-arm darts, as shown in Fig. 20, this section. For the waist-line tucks, which may be on the right or the wrong side, depending on the material and whether you wish them for decoration or not, make a fold on the line of tailor's tacks, baste, and then stitch each one ¼ inch from the fold for the length of the tuck. Tie all the thread ends securely. Make very narrow French seams along the shoulder of both the garment and the ruffle, following Art. 64 and Fig. 33, *Essential Stitches and Seams*, when they will appear on the wrong side as at *a* and *b*, Fig. 29, this section. Next, place two rows of gathering threads in the ruffle, as in Fig. 3, this section, draw it up to fit the edge to which it is to be attached, and baste and stitch it, as at *c*, Fig. 29, keeping the seam lines *a* and *b* exactly matching and tapering the seam to nothing at the ends, *d* and *e*. Tie the threads securely, and overcast the seam edges, as at *f*. Finish the under-arm seams with French seams, noting that the back is longer than the front because there are no under-arm darts in the back.

Trim away this extra back length, starting from the under-arm seam and trimming toward the centre back. Turn and baste the hem, as shown in Fig. 29, *Essential Stitches and Seams*, making this about 2 inches wide when finished—slip-stitching as shown if silk or rayon fabric, or machine stitching a service garment of cotton.

56. Finishing the Nightgown.—Join the strips of bias, and press open the seams. If you are using commercial bias, press open on fold so that the bias will appear as in Fig. 30, view (*a*). Baste around the neck line in the usual way, leaving about 1 inch of the bias free and starting near the back so that the final joining will not come in a conspicuous place. Baste to within ¼ inch of the first lapel corner, as at *a*. Then, holding the bias so that the edge of it comes flush with the corner, as at *b*, continue around the corner even with the other edge, as at *c*, and crease the binding on the direct bias so that the crease runs straight across the bias from side to side, as at *d*. Then bring the free edges together at the point where they exactly meet, as at *e*, and crease through the two thicknesses of the

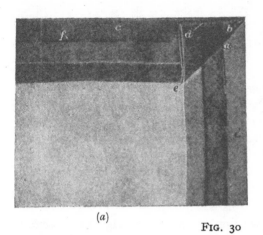

(*a*)

(*b*)

FIG. 30

binding from *b* to *e*. In binding that you make yourself, this crease will extend to the raw edges. Slip the needle through the two thicknesses of the binding at *a* and continue basting $\frac{1}{4}$ inch from the edge on the other side, as at *f*.

57. Continue basting down the centre-front opening, keeping the basting here, as at *a*, Fig. 31, and later the stitching *b*, in a straight line, but tapering the depth of the seam allowance out to the smallest possible amount at the point of the slash, as at *c*. Continue basting up around the second corner, handling it exactly like the first, and baste to within 1 inch of the beginning of the binding, remembering to hold the binding taut on rounded edges. Cut the bias on a straight thread so that the ends meet in a $\frac{1}{4}$-inch seam. Join this seam, press open, and then complete the basting.

FIG. 31

58. When replacing the basting around the corners with stitching, stitch to the point *a*, Fig. 30, view (*b*) ; then lift the presser foot, raise the needle out of the material, and pull the material just as though you were going to break the thread, but only far enough to bring out sufficient thread to make a loop that will go over the fold of the bind

ing at the corner, as at *b*. Then turn this fold in the opposite direction, insert the needle $\frac{1}{4}$ inch from the second edge and as near as possible to point *a* where the last stitch ended, and continue the stitching $\frac{1}{4}$ inch from the second edge, as at *c*.

Turn the bias back to the wrong side, turn in the free edge, if it is not already turned, baste, and slip-stitch in place, forming neat, diagonal folds from the corners to the edge of the binding and keeping both sides of the binding as nearly alike as possible. Bind the ruffled arm-hole edges as usual. From your binding material, make a small bow as an ornament for the centre front, making this straight like a belt, or, if you are using commercial binding, folding this double and stitching it close to the edge. Stitch, turn, and press the belt as directed for straps in Art. 11, this section, and then tack it in place at the under-arm seams.

REVERSIBLE KIMONO

59. A singular charm, due partly to its simplicity and partly to its grace of line, characterizes the reversible negligèe kimono, shown in Fig. 32. The reversible idea, besides simplify-ing the making, adds to the wear-

FIG. 32

ability of the garment, particularly when dark and light colours are combined for the most practical effect. The model illustrated was developed of a print having a brilliant red motif on a black ground, and a lining repeating the print colour.

60. Material Requirements.—Silk or rayon, crêpe satin, or similar weaves that are not bulky are recommended for this garment, since two thicknesses are used throughout. For warmth, thin flannel, or a light-weight wool crêpe may be lined with a contrasting silk crêpe. Of any fabric, 3 yards of each colour is needed for the average size.

61. Cutting the Kimono.—Cut both thicknesses of the kimono exactly alike, according to the directions that follow. These may be varied to suit the small, medium, or large figure, these three sizes being quite sufficient for a kimono of this type.

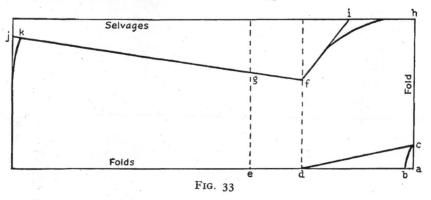

FIG. 33

Fold the material through the lengthwise centre, then again through the crosswise centre, making four thicknesses, and pin securely. Place the folded material on your cutting table with the lengthwise folds next you and the crosswise fold to your right, as shown in Fig. 33.

Call the corner at the lower right a, and from it measure to the left I inch and mark b, and 3 inches above it on the crosswise fold and mark c. These points are the same for all sizes. From a, measure to the left 14 inches for the small, 15 inches for the medium, and 16 inches for the large figure, and mark d. With your yardstick as a guide, mark a line straight up from d to the selvages, as indicated. From d, mark e 7 inches to the left, and indicate a line straight up to the selvages from e, as shown. On the line from d, measure 10 inches for the small, $11\frac{1}{2}$ inches for the medium, and $13\frac{1}{2}$ inches for the large figure, and mark f. From e, measure up 11 inches for the small, $12\frac{1}{2}$ inches for the medium, and 14 inches for the large figure, and mark g. Mark the upper right corner h, measure to the left along the selvages 9 inches, and mark i, this measure being the same for all sizes. Mark a point midway between h and i.

With the aid of your yardstick, connect *i* and *f* and *c* and *d* with straight lines. Then place, your yardstick so that its edge touches *f* and *g* and indicate a straight line that will pass through both these points and extend to the cut edges of the material. Consider its end *j* and mark a point, *k*, 1 inch above *j*. In large sizes, point *j* may extend beyond the selvages and a piecing would then have to be used to increase the width at the lower edge.

62. From 4 inches from *j* on the lower edges, cut through all thick-, nesses to *k*, to *f* through *g*, and from *f* toward *i*, curving off the point, as shown, to the midway point between *i* and *h*. Now, cut from *b* to *c* through all thicknesses, but when *c* is reached, open up the cross-wise fold, and, for the front neck line, cut from *c* to *d* through the two upper thicknesses only, and through the top fold from *d* to the open edge for the front opening. Cut the lining similarly.

If you desire a slightly more fitted garment, trim away 1 inch from the back at point *f*, graduating to nothing above and below.

63. Making the Kimono.—First baste, then stitch the under-arm seams of both inner and outer sections, stitching from the top down on each side about 1 inch, then, skipping 1 inch, and continuing to the bottom. This open space is to take care of the belt. Tie all thread ends securely, and press the seams open. Although as a rule, checking up on fitting features should be unnecessary in a garment of this type, because it has been cut to measure and is also adjustable to the figure, nevertheless, it is a good plan at this time to slip the parts of the kimono on separately, if for nothing more than to make sure of the length. The real reason for this is, that the stitching and pressing of the under-arm seams may have caused them to become stretched. Slip on the outside portion of the kimono, lap it as you would wish to wear it and pin as lapped. Then examine its lower edge, and if it appears longer at the side seams, mark a new line to correspond with the remainder of the kimono length. Remove and try on the lining, lapping it exactly as you did the outside portion, and mark the lower edge here also. If the outside and the inside are both made of the same type of material, they will usually appear about the same, when made of different weaves, there may be more or less stretching at the under-arm.

Next, place the two thicknesses together, right sides in, outside edges and under-arm seams matching. First, carefully pin, then baste, and stitch around certain parts of the outside edges, following the new line at the under-arms if changes were necessary here. For all the remaining stitching use the regulation ⅜ inch seam allowance. Do not stitch around the edges of the cape sleeves at this time, also leave an 8 to 10 inch space unstitched at the lower centre back edge. Trim off any excess seam allowances, then press the joining where possible to keep the finished edge sharp, and turn to the right side by drawing the entire garment through the opening along the seam at the lower back.

To finish the outside edges of the cape sleeves, it is necessary to draw each one singly back through the seam opening. When one has been carefully drawn through, pin the lining and the outer portion of the kimono accurately together, edges meeting entirely around the capelet, then baste and stitch as for a plain seam. Tie the thread ends, press the seam open, and push the capelet back in place. Do the same at the other arm opening.

Now turn the edges of the lower back opening toward each other, baste, and continue to baste around the outside and capelet edges of the kimono. Then slip-stitch the edges of the opening together, press, and remove the bastings.

From the material remaining along the side seams, cut two dark and two light strips of the proper length and 1½ to 1¾ inches wide. Baste one light and one dark strip together, stitch, turn, baste along the edges, and press. With the back seam edges of one under-arm opening turned toward each other, insert the raw end of a belt tie, dark side out, between the two thicknesses of the back and slip-stitch securely in place. Merely slip-stitch the two front edges together. ·Treat the other tie belt similarly.

If a secure closing is wanted at the front, sew a snap fastener of a fairly good size there, first determining its position by trying on the kimono and lapping it the desired amount. Also, if preferred, the tie belt may be entirely omitted, and the closing effected by means of a narrow tie underneath, in the manner of a coat closing, and the snap fastener on top.

EASY GARMENT MAKING

EXAMINATION QUESTIONS

(1) What is the advantage of using two rows of gathering when arranging fulness ?

(2) What should be the relative position of the crosswise and lengthwise threads when making the first fold in preparation for cutting bias strips ?

(3) Describe the method to be followed when fitting the panties.

(4) What materials are most satisfactory for slips, and why ?

(5) Describe the procedure for marking the skirt length of a garment for one's self, if one must do this without assistance.

(6) Describe the basting of the hip darts used in the overblouse.

(7) Tell how to determine the amount of material necessary to make a nightgown like that shown in Fig. 27.

(8) Submit a sampler showing a joining in a bias strip cut from striped material.

(9) Submit a sampler showing the method of marking, basting, and stitching darts as shown in Fig. 20.

PLEASE NOTICE

Now that you have completed your reports for *Essential Stitches and Seams* and *Easy Garment Making*, we want you to make one of the garments shown in this book and send it to us for inspection. Procure your material, following the suggestions given for the garment you decide to make. Then, follow the directions carefully, doing the work to the best of your ability. Send your finished garment to us, so that we may judge your ability to apply the sewing principles taught in these first two lessons. We shall examine it carefully, give you any suggestions or advice you need to improve your work, and return your garment, which we hope you will enjoy and be proud to wear.

We do want to be sure that you can make a correct buttonhole because it is an important detail in sewing work. So, if you have made a garment that does not require a buttonhole, please send us a sampler of a finished buttonhole made according to the instructions in *Essential Stitches and Seams*.

INDIVIDUALIZING TISSUE-PAPER PATTERNS

NATURE AND DEVELOPMENT

NATURE OF PATTERNS

1. A pattern is a guide with which to cut out garments, a help that simplifies their making and gives the assistance that every sewer, from the beginner to the most expert, can use to advantage. A well-cut, modern commerical pattern also has real educational value, for an understanding of the lines of commercial as well as drafted patterns and a knowledge of the relation of these lines to one another help immeasurably in both fitting and designing. Therefore, it is very much to the advantage of the dressmaking student to regard each pattern as a valuable aid to sewing progress, to study every one used in order to become thoroughly familiar with the outline of each section and to learn to recognize, at a glance, the various parts and their use in a pattern as a whole.

2. Commercial Patterns.—By the term *commercial pattern* is meant that type of pattern which is manufactured in standard sizes by various companies engaged in this business, and available all over the world through sales agencies or from the main office of the company. Such patterns are generally made of thin paper to avoid bulk and include a section for every part of the garment, properly marked and notched to simplify cutting and putting together. Frequently, several variations of the original design are added to make the pattern more versatile. Properly assembled and folded, the various pattern pieces are inserted in an envelope of convenient size, one side of which always shows an illustration of the garment and its variations, the other, or reverse side, generally having sizes and yardage requirements listed. Frequently, small illustrations of the various pattern pieces, properly identified, are shown on the back of the envelope so that the user can tell without opening it of how many pieces the pattern consists, their sizes and shapes, and in this way form an idea of the elaborateness of the design and the amount of work that will be needed to complete it.

Needless to say, these patterns are fashion aids of the greatest importance, reflecting each season the latest fashion trends and thus spreading much of the news of the fashion world. Naturally, however, care must be used in selecting them, both for chic and for becomingness. The ability to do this seems instinctive in some, but it can be acquired and fostered by study and observation, as you will learn as you proceed with your Course.

3.   Drafted Patterns.—Foundation patterns, individually developed to a set of personal, balanced measurements, are called *drafts*. In contrast to the commercial pattern, they have practically no fashion value, except that they should follow the silhouette of the season. Generally made up in heavy paper, they find considerable use as foundations for designing, as cutting guides for simple garments and as test patterns for checking purposes. The drafted pattern is really the foundation for all commercial pattern work, and the person who has mastered a particular system of drafting has provided a fine groundwork of pattern knowledge. Blouses, sleeves, skirts, dresses, undergarments, and wraps may be drafted.

PATTERN DEVELOPMENT

4.   Origin of Commercial Patterns.—From a very humble beginning in the home of Ebenezer and Ellen Butterick in the year 1863, the manufacture of commercial patterns has become a major industry. To Butterick, a country tailor, his wife, after completing a dress for one of her children, made the suggestion that women would undoubtedly be interested in having patterns to aid them in making clothes for their children. He was struck at once with the practical features of the idea, so he and his wife set about to devise plans whereby they could produce and supply patterns for this need. The first pattern put on the market by them in Fitchburg, Mass., was very crude, simple in form, and made of heavy paper. But, encouraged by their success, the two pioneers expanded and improved their product, thus laying the foundation for a business that has grown and developed to include patterns for practically all types of garments in every wanted size.

5. Advancement in Patterns.—Aided by a large style organization in every fashion centre of the world, pattern manufacturers wield a far-reaching influence on fashion. And they have worked out a plan whereby patterns have been brought within the reach of every woman interested in sewing. Because of the mass production necessary, tissue-paper patterns must, of course, be standardized. And this feature makes them somewhat limiting for those women who vary from the average in figure as well as those who possess original ideas and want designs suitable and becoming just to themselves. However, commercial patterns have so many excellent features and prove so adaptable in the hands of those who understand how to handle them that their value should not be overlooked.

6. Purpose of Lesson.—To prepare you to use patterns with the greatest of ease and success is the aim of this lesson. The instruction it contains will open up new roads to achievement in their use and make them just that much more valuable to you. Teaching you how to alter a pattern to suit the individual and how to develop a perfect-fitting foundation pattern, as it does, it will prove a valuable and useful aid to successful dressmaking, particularly for those who must depend on others for fitting.

PRODUCTION AND DISTRIBUTION
AIDS TO CORRECT USE

7. As commercial patterns have developed, their value has increased, and they are now as complete and efficient as the skill and ingenuity of their manufacturers can make them. The first patterns consisted merely of the outline sections of a garment, namely, the back, the front, and the sleeve. At the present time, however, they are often cut into intricate pieces, and seam allowances, trimming details, all inside seams, in fact, all possible aids to efficiency of use are indicated on the pattern pieces. All of these helps should be thoroughly understood and followed.

8. Seam Allowances.—Most pattern companies include a seam allowance on the various pieces of their patterns. The majority use the standard ⅜-inch seam allowance, although some manufacturers consider a greater allowance, from ½ inch to 1½ inches, particularly along the under-arm seam, necessary for fitting and make this provision. Before cutting out a garment with the aid of a pattern, it is well to investigate the width of the seam allowance and consider it in connection with the material to be used and the type of seam desired. For instance, ⅜ inch is sufficient for a regulation plain seam, unless the material frays easily. For certain types of tailored seams, such as a side skirt seam on which a tailored placket opening is to be made, a greater allowance, up to 1 to 1½ inches, is essential and must be provided when cutting.

9. Perforations and Markings.—To make the cutting and construction of garments easier and to produce the best results, perforations or printed directions are used on patterns. For instance, the proper placement of the pattern on the material is directed entirely by *perforations*, or small holes. Certain ones, usually triple, indicate that the pattern edge should be placed on a fold ; others indicate darts, pleats, or shirrings ; still others mark the location of trimming details. Also, pattern pieces are marked with perforations or arrows to indicate how they should be placed as regards the straight of the material, for, unless the grain of the fabric is correct in all parts of the garment, it will neither set nor look well.

10. *Notches* are used in the edge of pattern pieces to aid in the joining of the various sections. These are very accurately placed and should be marked on the fabric before the pattern is removed and then very carefully matched in the making of the garment.

11. The *printed tissue-paper pattern* contains printed lines that indicate the manner in which the pieces should be placed on the material. Also, printed directions take the place of all perforations necessary in patterns that are not printed, thereby simplifying their use.

12. Directions for Use.—Accompanying each pattern is a sheet containing complete directions for the use of the pattern. This will make clear for you the meaning of every perforation and marking, and its key list of the pattern pieces will help you to recognize each piece and to understand its position as part of the garment.

When the various pattern pieces have been studied, the manner of placing them on the material should next engage your attention. Layouts for practically all widths of material and all of the pattern sizes are given. So, no matter what the fabric or the size, illustrations of how to place the pattern for the best advantage in cutting and for the best effect in the finished garment, are given.

Also included are directions for putting the garment together, as well as illustrations with instructions for certain details of making and finishing. These, as well as the cutting layouts, represent a great deal of work on the part of the pattern companies. So they should be referred to at all stages in the making of the garment, and their information carefully applied.

13. Variations in Design.—Another service that many manufacturers supply is a means of varying collars, sleeves, certain trimming details, and even more important parts of the design. In many cases, the variations are such that one gives a more tailored effect than the other. Thus, when developed in different colours and fabrics, two quite dissimilar models may be made from the same cutting guide. As can readily be understood, patterns of this kind effect considerable saving.

SIZING OF PATTERNS

14. The matter of size in a pattern is of vast importance, so manufacturers of patterns treat this feature very thoroughly. Naturally, it is to their advantage to have their patterns true to measure as well as suited in size to as many figure types as possible. So, to make patterns as efficient as possible, they have worked out accurate systems whereby the gradation from one pattern size to the next is kept regular as well as suited to the figure changes. This is known as *grading*, and is considered a very important feature in the manufacture of patterns.

15. From the standpoint of design also, the sizing of patterns is important. For instance, a person who purchases a pattern in the size she requires expects that its lines will be suited to her figure. The pattern companies, keeping this in mind, make up patterns in size ranges that are suitable to the silhouette of the design. Slenderizing fashions, for example, are available in size 36 upward, sometimes to 54, while definitely youthful fashions can be had in size ranges from

11 to 17 or 12 to 20. Average-type patterns have a much wider size range, these being procurable, as a rule, from 32 to 44.

PURCHASING PATTERNS

16. Availability.—Practically all department stores maintain a pattern counter, where the patterns of one or several of the manufacturers are offered for sale. Fashion publications for current styles, as well as counter or stock books, which illustrate all the patterns available by the company publishing them, may be seen at the counters and selections made from them. Mail-order service is offered by all pattern companies also.

17. Importance of Correct Size.—Too much emphasis cannot be laid on the selection of patterns of the correct size. Otherwise considerable alteration will be necessary, and this, besides requiring a great deal of time, is likely to destroy the style and balance of the design. Before a pattern is purchased, therefore, one's measurements must be taken with great care.

Practically all patterns are developed with an ideal figure as a standard, that of an average, well-formed woman, so they do not approach perfection in fit for all types. However, they are usually graded up and down from a 36 bust and a 39 hip, these being the two measurements that are considered fundamental. Consequently, the bust and the hip size must be correctly measured and a pattern that approximates as nearly as possible one or the other obtained for the best results.

18. Measurements for Pattern Sizes.—As a rule, the actual bust measure is considered as the pattern size for dresses, blouses, coats, negligées, slips, nightgowns, pyjamas, brassières, and combinations. The hip or waist measure is taken when a pattern for a skirt, shorts, panties, or a petticoat is wanted. The breast measure or the age is the standard for children's patterns.

Patterns are generally available in even sizes, that is, 34, 36, 38, etc., although special types, or those designed for out-of-proportion figures can be procured in uneven sizes. Patterns for children and misses, in many cases, are available in uneven as well as even breast sizes and ages.

19. Size of Pattern to Select.—For the majority of patterns, the size to purchase is usually determined by the bust measure. However, exceptions must be made in certain cases, for at times a pattern smaller or larger than the bust size is a wiser choice than one that actually corresponds to the bust measure.

20. A pattern smaller than the bust size should generally be purchased by the person whose bust is large in proportion to her other measurements. This is usually the small-boned type, whose width of back and width of chest are comparatively small in relation to the bust. It can readily be understood that a smaller size pattern will fit the neck line, shoulders, and armhole, while the necessary alterations to enlarge the bust section can easily be made.

21. When it is found necessary to purchase a pattern large than the bust size, the reverse is generally true, that is, the chest and width of back are large in proportion to the bust size. The type requiring this variation from the usual, is generally the thin or athletic person who has a comparatively large frame but very little excess fat. Her width at the shoulders needs the larger size to insure a good fit through the upper part of the body, while the necessary alteration to make the garment small enough through the bust can be taken care of when preparing the pattern before cutting.

22. There is still another type of figure that requires a special rule in pattern-size selection and that is the one whose bust and hips are completely out of proportion. The more usual variation shows a hip size large in proportion to the bust, but the reverse is sometimes true. Such figures, when preparing a guide pattern, should select separate blouse and skirt patterns in order to obtain the proper bust size in the waist and the proper hip size in the skirt, although if but one can be provided, select the size most likely to fit the neck and shoulders.

23. Any out-of-proportion type should give special thought to the selection of her dress-pattern size. For instance, if a design with an intricately cut skirt is wanted, it should be selected in the proper hip size, for it is practically impossible to alter successfully an elaborately pieced style. If the waist section is of more elaborate construction than the rest of the dress, select the dress pattern by the bust size and do the necessary alteration on the simpler portion of the pattern.

PREPARATION AND USE OF GUIDE PATTERNS

VALUE AND USES

24. Meaning of Guide Pattern.—Since very few of us who use patterns are perfectly proportioned, it is necessary to have garments made with commercial patterns fitted to our figures by means of alterations and adjustments. The poorly fitted one neither looks nor wears well, it is completely without style, and it is bound to have an amateurish look. A great deal of this difficulty, however, may be overcome by the use of a foundation pattern, sometimes called a *guide* or *permanent pattern*.

By the term foundation, or guide, pattern is meant a perfectly plain pattern, either in one-piece effect or with a joining at the waist line, depending on fashion, which has been cut from muslin or some similar trial material, carefully fitted to the figure according to the current style silhouette, and altered where necessary. With the alterations complete, the pattern itself is made to conform to the fitted muslin model. Then, for permanency, another one is cut from heavy but flexible paper that will wear well and stand considerable handling.

25. Uses of a Guide Pattern.—If you sew for yourself and must depend for fitting on others, who are usually inexperienced, a correctly prepared guide pattern can become one of your most valuable assets. Perhaps its greatest service to you will be as a check on any pattern you plan to use, assuring you even before you cut out a garment that its shoulder length will be correct, its sleeves will look well, its waist line will be exactly right for your figure, not too high nor too low, in fact, that its effect generally will be just what you want and have previously been striving for without success. You will find the foundation pattern also a valuable aid in designing, such a pattern being a requirement for flat-pattern work. Then, too, it may even be used as a cutting guide for simple garments. Considering the comparatively small amount of time that goes into the preparation of such a pattern, its usefulness and helpfulness, both in doing creative work and in saving effort, are very great in proportion.

SELECTION OF PATTERN

26. The first requisite for a successful guide pattern is an enthusiastic interest on the part of the person making it, an attitude of firm conviction that the completed pattern will prove to be a valuable and helpful aid in dressmaking. Then, there should be the determination to be most accurate in measurements, pattern alteration, cutting, basting, fitting, and finishing. A state of mind that embraces interest and determination is bound to produce successful results.

27. Type of Pattern to Select.—A very important feature of a successful foundation pattern is the guide that is used for cutting it. Naturally, a pattern that is too elaborate in cut, or one that does not very nearly approximate your measurements will be burdensome to prepare and tedious to fit. On the other hand, if care and thought are given to the selection of the pattern, much of the difficulty is overcome at the start. It is most important, therefore, that you select the proper type of pattern, namely, a dress of simple lines, having, if possible, a plain waist with a normal shoulder and armhole line, a regulation neck line, close-fitting long sleeves, and a two-piece skirt, or one that can be altered to produce these features.

The pattern may consist of a waist front and back, a skirt front and back, and a sleeve, or, when Fashion favours the one-piece garment, a dress front and back will take the place of the waist and skirt sections. It is a good plan in any season to make both types, that is, a guide having a waist-line joining as well as one in one piece ; but if only one is being planned for, the one with a waist-line joining is to be preferred. In Fig. 1 is shown the ideal pattern, including waist front (*a*), waist back (*b*), sleeve (*c*), skirt front (*d*), and skirt back (*e*).

It is not always possible to find cutting guides of the necessary simplicity, but it is a comparatively easy matter to eliminate pleats or fullness, also trimming details that do not affect the foundation lines. With this thought in mind, study the pattern books and select a particular guide that has the proper foundation lines at shoulder, neck line, and armhole and that will lend itself readily to such changes as are necessary to have the final pattern follow in its outlines as closely as possible the various sections shown in Fig. 1. Be sure to purchase it in the size best suited to your figure.

28. Characteristics of Pattern Pieces.—To become familiar with the fundamental differences between the various pattern sections, it will be well for you to study these sections carefully. In comparing the front and back, Fig. 1, views (a) and (b), notice that the neck curve of the front is deeper than that of the back, the shoulder line of the front is, or should be, by actual measurement $\frac{1}{2}$ inch shorter than the back, the front armhole curve is deeper than the back, and there is an essential dart in the front, either from the shoulder line or the under arm, while in the back, the dart, if one is used, is from the neck line. The waist line of the front curves downward, while that of the back is straight or has a slightly inward curve. Also, the front waist is wider than the back.

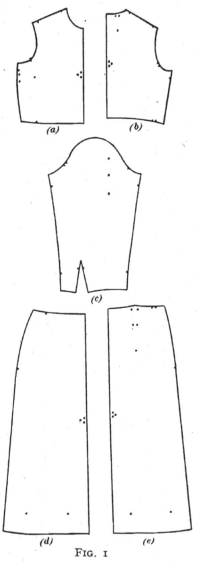

FIG. 1

29. To recognize the front from the back of a sleeve, notice the armhole curves in view (c), one of which is always somewhat higher than the other. The high curve, which may be readily found, if in doubt, by folding the sleeve pattern through the lengthwise centre, is always the back of the sleeve. Another means of identifying the back of the sleeve is by the elbow dart, if it is present, or a dart from the wrist, both of which are always on the back. In certain sleeves, the wrist line curves downward from front to back.

30. As to the skirt, the waist-line curve of the front, view (d), is always deeper than that of the back, view (e). The front is generally wider than the back at the waist, although they may be the same width below. If there is a front dart extending downward from the waist line, it is much narrower than the back dart. As a rule, however, there is a dart in the back only.

METHOD OF TAKING MEASUREMENTS

31. Importance of Proper Measurements.—To purchase a pattern, it is necessary to know only the bust, waist, and hip measures to select the proper size, but to alter a pattern, in order to have it conform as nearly as possible to your individual figure, naturally much more is required. Directions, therefore, are given for properly measuring various parts of the figure, and these must be followed definitely for good results. This is especially true when the figure is out of proportion ; but it is true of practically all figures, for there are very few sets of measurements, even though they are in good proportion, that really correspond exactly to the ideal measurements on which tissue-paper or commercial patterns are necessarily based.

The best results can be obtained if figure measurements are compared with pattern-measurements by placing the tape measure in approximately the same positions on the figure as on the pattern. Careful study of Figs. 2 and 3, which indicate clearly the relation of figure measures with pattern measures, will be a definite help to you. In Fig. 2, view (a) shows the human figure with the various pattern pieces placed against it and the position that the pattern lines would take when so arranged. View (b) shows the pattern of the waist front, (c) the skirt front, and (d) the sleeve, with the various pattern lines indicated on them also. In Fig. 3, view (a), the back view of the figure is shown, at (b) the back-waist section, and at (c) the back skirt with pattern lines marked here also.

32. Measurements for Pattern Use.—In order to use patterns with the greatest success, you should understand not only the position that the pattern lines ought to assume on the figure, but also the way to take measurements and to apply them in adjusting the pattern to meet individual requirements. First of all then, become familiar with all the foundation and seam lines of the pattern ; next, follow out in detail the instructions in regard to the taking of measurements, and study them in relation to the foundation pattern lines. Then, if any changes are necessary to make the patterns correspond to your figure, these can be made successfully by following the instructions.

The measurements required for altering patterns and likewise for fitting and making garments of different types are those used by pattern drafters in preparation for the manufacture of waist, sleeve, and skirt patterns and include those in the following list.

1. Bust   3. Hip   5. Shoulder Length   7. Armhole
2. Waist   4. Neck   6. Width of Chest   8. Front-Waist Length
9. Width of Back.
10. Length of Back
11. Inside Sleeve Length
12. Upper Arm
13. Wrist
14. Skirt Dart
15. Front-Skirt Length
16. Full-Front Length
17 Side-Skirt Length
18. Back-Skirt Length
19. Full-Back Length

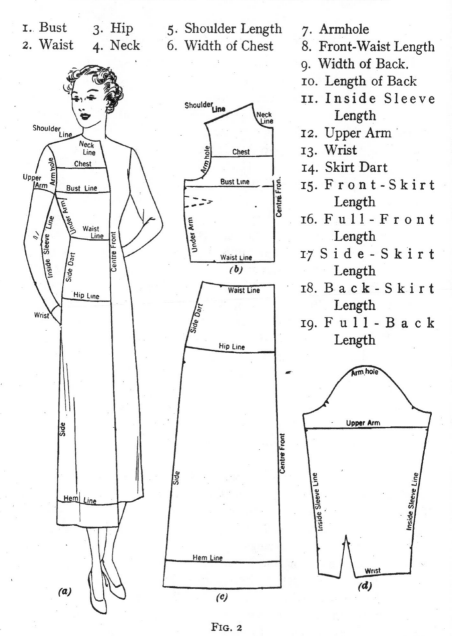

Fig. 2

While it is true that but one or two of these measures, and in some cases none at all, may be needed for the alterations you will be required to make, nevertheless you would not be able to know how closely the pattern you are using conforms to your size unless you checked it first with all these measures. You will find, too, that as you gain experience and become thoroughly familiar with your own mea-sures, you will not need to make such complete tests when you know that only a slight change will be required. The beginner, however, cannot be too painstaking for good results.

33. A v e r a g e Measurements. — So that the beginner in dressmaking may become familiar with the different measure-ments and their rela-tive proportion to one another, Table I, in which are listed the standard body mea-surements used in de-veloping patterns, is given here. This table will guide you in tak-ing measurements, for, by considering the proportion of related measurements in the table, you will be able to determine whether the corresponding measurements you take are in propor-

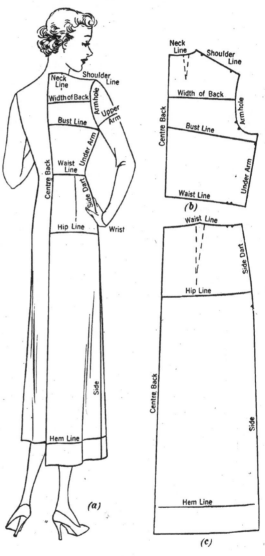

Fig. 3

tion. For instance, the chest, shoulder length, and width of back should be considered in relation to the bust measure, while the front- and back-waist lengths need be considered only in rela-tion to each other, for these two measures depend more on the height of the figure and the position of the waist line than they do on the bust measure, although a proportionately long front-waist length may, at times, be caused by a large bust.

34. Skirt-length measures depend largely on height and therefore are not included in the table. A point to keep in mind when taking them, however, is that the regulation figure will have a back-skirt length 1 inch longer than the front and a side length ½ inch longer than the front and the same amount shorter than the back. Variations from this rule usually mean that alterations will be required in your skirt pattern for they indicate prominent hips or abdomen or, perhaps, a sway-back figure.

35. Importance of Accuracy.—In order to illustrate exactly the position of the tape measure on the figure when the various measurements are being taken, and also the proper procedure, detailed illustrations and instructions are given, for too much stress cannot be laid on the necessity for accuracy and correctness in this work. Study the illustrations, therefore, before you start. Then, as you take each measurement, check the position of the tape line with the position shown, and check the result also with the table of proportionate measurements.

Use a good tape measure, one that is not worn and old, for tape measures are quite likely to stretch with use. It is a wise precaution

TABLE I

AVERAGE PROPORTION OF MEASUREMENTS IN INCHES

Bust	Waist	Hip	Neck	Shoulder Length	Width of Chest	Armhole	Front-Waist Length	Width of Back	Length of Back	Inside Sleeve Length	Upper Arm	Wrist	Side Dart
30	26	33	12½	4⅜	12	14½	14	12¾	14½	16	10	6¼	6½
32	27	35	13	4½	12½	14⅞	14½	13¼	15	16½	10½	6½	6½
34	28	37	13½	4⅝	13¼	15¼	15	13¾	15½	16½	11	6¾	6¾
36	30	39	14	4¾	13¾	15⅝	15¼	14¼	15¾	17	11½	7	7
38	32	41	14½	4⅞	14¼	16	15½	14¾	16	17½	12	7¼	7
40	34	43	15	5	14¾	16⅜	15¾	15¼	16¼	18	12½	7½	7
42	36	45	15½	5⅛	15¼	16¾	16	15¾	16½	18	13	7¾	7
44	38	47½	16	5¼	15¾	17⅛	16¼	16¼	16⅝	18	13½	8	7
46	40	50	16½	5⅜	16¼	17½	16½	16¾	16¾	18	14	8¼	7½
48	42	53	17	5½	16¾	17⅞	16¾	17¼	16⅞	18	14½	8½	7¾
50	44	56	17½	5⅝	17¼	18¼	17	17¾	17	18	15	8¾	8

to compare the tape measure with a ruler or yard-stick to make sure that it is accurate.

Practice in taking measurements is of great advantage to beginners. Take the measurements of several different figures and also the measurements of one figure two or three times in order to appreciate the importance of placing the measuring tape correctly, and thus getting the measurements the same each time.

36. Figure Preparation and Posture.—When measurements are being taken, the figure should be properly corseted, provided a restraining garment is generally worn. Also, the dress should be without excessive fullness or bulk at any particular place, and, if possible, should be of the set-in sleeve type, for the position of the armhole and the length of the shoulder seam of the garment will prove helpful in determining the exact position of the tape in each case. The person being measured should stand erect, on both feet, and in natural manner and should let her arms hang straight at her sides, unless the measurement being taken requires a different position for the arms.

37. Use of Mirror.—As it is practically impossible to take your own measurements with any degree of accuracy, it is advisable to have some one do this for you. But first instruct this person as to how each measurement should be taken. A good plan is to stand before a mirror and to read aloud the directions for placing the tape.

If you must do your own measuring, do it as carefully as possible and with the aid of a mirror. While you may not be able to take all of your measurements, you can at least determine the ones most essential when making simple pattern alterations.

38. Placing Guide Tape.—As an aid in measuring, arrange a tape around the waist line of the person to be measured. It may be an extra tape measure, or a length of twilled tape, but it should be pinned snugly around the normal waist line and follow the natural line of the figure, that is, have a slight downward slant in front. The position of this tape will be a guide in taking the length measurements of both waist and skirt.

39. Procedure in Taking Measurements.—In Figs. 4 and 5, the position in which the tape measure should be placed for each of the various measurements is clearly shown and numbered. In addition, detailed instructions, designated by the same number, follow. Constant reference to the illustrations and to the rules will aid you in obtaining perfect results.

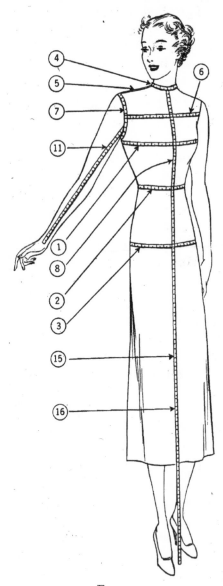

FIG. 4

Take the *bust measure* (1) over the fullest part of the bust and the fullest part of the shoulder blades, giving the tape a slight upward slant toward the back. This measure should be easy enough to allow two fingers to be slipped under the tape, but still should not be loose.

Take the *waist measure* (2) in approximately the same position as the guide tape. This is a close, rather snug measurement.

Take the *hip measure* (3) approximately 7 inches below the waist-line tape. If the fullest part of the hips comes either above or below the 7-inch point, measure the hips at their largest part. Draw the tape smoothly around the figure without pulling it tight and keep it in line with the waist-line tape, that is, with a slight downward slant toward the front.

Take the *neck measure* (4) by placing the tape around the base of the neck, inside the collar if the person being measured is wearing one. Take this measurement closely, but not so tight that the tape will bind.

Take the *shoulder length* (5) in approximately the position that the shoulder seam of a garment would take, that is, from the neck to the tip of the shoulder bone, just on top of the shoulder. Since a properly placed shoulder seam should not be visible when the figure is looked at either from the direct back or the direct front, take care to have the tape correctly placed, that is, extending outward from a point directly behind the ear to the tip of the shoulder joint.

Take the *width of chest* (6) by measuring smoothly across the chest from the point on one side where the arm joins the body to a corresponding point on the opposite side. Be very careful not to have this measurement too wide nor yet too narrow, for it would be just as incorrect to have the front section of your garment extend over on to the arm, a common fault, as to have a drawn effect here, as would result if the sleeve were set too far in on the waist front.

FIG. 5

Take the *armhole measure* (7) by placing the tape around under the arm, bringing it close to the body, and then up around the arm to the shoulder point. Do not draw the tape measure tight as this should be an easy measure.

Take the *front-waist length* (8) by measuring from the hollow at the base of the throat to the guide tape at the waist line. This should be an easy measure.

Take the *width of back* (9) by measuring across the shoulder blades from one armhole point to the other, placing the tape measure in relatively the same position in back as it was in front for the width of chest.

Take the *length of back* (10) by measuring from the prominent bone at the base of the neck vertically downward to the waist-line tape.

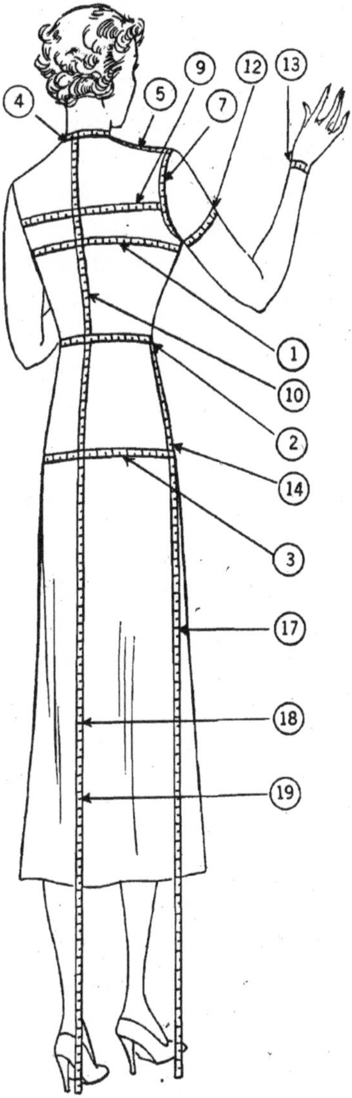

Take the *inside sleeve length* (11) by measuring from the hollow of the under arm to the wrist in line with the thumb, having the arm held away from the body.

Take the *upper-arm measure* (12) by measuring easily around the fullest part of the arm above the elbow.

Take the *wrist measure* (13) by measuring closely around the wrist.

Take the *skirt-dart measure* (14) by measuring from the waist line at the side vertically down to the fullest part of the hips.

Take the *front-skirt length* (15) by measuring from the tape around the waist vertically down to the floor at the centre front.

Take the *full-front length* (16) from the hollow at the base of the throat down over the bust to the waist line and then down to the floor.

Take the *side-skirt length* (17) by measuring directly at the side from the tape around the waist down to the floor.

Take the *back-skirt length* (18) by measuring from the tape around the waist down to the floor at the centre-back.

Take the *full-back length* (19) by measuring from the prominent bone at the back of the neck line to the waist line and then down to the floor.

PREPARING THE PATTERN
PRELIMINARY WORK

40. Accuracy in measuring, cutting, and adjusting is the most important point in pattern alteration and must characterize every step of the work if good results are to be obtained. And, since the main reason for making pattern changes is improvement in fitting, the necessity for exactness in every operation becomes apparent. It is well, therefore, for you to take ample time for the work, both to consider the alterations and to make them. Never slash into a pattern hastily, but rather think well over each change, first marking it and visualizing, if possible, what effect a particular position will have in relation to the result you desire, and then cutting, measuring, and adjusting carefully.

41. Removing Unnecessary Features.—If your cutting guide has some style features, such as pleats, allowances for lapping, and so on, all of these should be cut away, folded back, or adjusted in such a way as to have the finished outline of your pattern similar to that shown in Fig. 1. If pleats are allowed for in the interior of the pattern, fold them in, following the perforations exactly, and pin securely in place. If the allowance has been made at the centre front or centre back, fold the pattern on the marked centre-front or centre-back line, or, if you prefer, trim away the allowance beyond the centre lines. Allowances for lapping also must be eliminated, either by folding back or cutting so that the centre lines will be on the edge of the pattern and make it possible to place the centre front or centre back exactly on the fold of the material.

However, if you wish to keep your original pattern intact, all of these allowances may merely be folded in, and a new pattern cut for use in the altering process. When such a pattern is cut, remember to transfer accurately to it all perforations and notches.

42. Removing Seam Allowances.—To simplify the process of measuring and altering, it is a good plan to trim away all seam allowances from the cutting guide that you are going to use in making your foundation pattern. The removal of the seam allowances enables you to work with the actual pattern size, gives the seam, or stitching, line its true importance, and prevents confusion in the mind by eliminating the $\frac{3}{8}$-inch allowance from your calculations as well as from the pattern. So, first of all, examine the pattern and its direction sheet for information as to the seam allowance made. If a greater allowance than the usual $\frac{3}{8}$ inch has been made, it, too, should be entirely trimmed away. For the greatest accuracy, measure the depth of the seam allowance along all the pattern edges and mark a continuous line with pencil to indicate the seam line. Then cut on the marked line.

43. Marking Foundation Lines.—As a further preparation for testing patterns by measurement to determine the amount of alteration needed, it is well to mark certain of the foundation lines, including the bust, hip, and upper-arm lines. These will represent on the pattern the approximate position of the tape line on the figure when the measurements are being taken, and, in certain cases, will also represent the straight crosswise grain of the garment fabric.

As shown in Fig. 2, view (b), draw the bust line on the blouse front at right angles to the centre front so that it passes through the under-arm line about $1\frac{1}{2}$ inches below the armhole line, or armscye. Then, place the back section next to the front so that both under-arm lines touch from the armhole for about $1\frac{1}{2}$ inches, pin in this position to a paper underneath, and continue the drawing of the bust line, as in Fig. 3, view (b). This will give it an upward slant toward the centre back similar to the position of the tape line when taking this measure.

Draw the hip line by measuring down from the waist line the side-dart measure in several places and marking points. Then, connect these points, as in Fig. 2, view (c), and Fig. 3, view (c), giving a curved effect to the line drawn on the pattern. Finally, as in Fig. 2, view (d), draw a horizontal line across the sleeve, just below the sleeve cap, corresponding to the upper-arm measurement.

44. Measuring the Pattern.—While the measurements of the figure are very important, the proper method of measuring the pattern means a great deal also. Study Figs. 2, 3, 4, and 5 with care first; then, using the tape measure accurately, place it on the pattern pieces so that you are actually measuring the same place on the pattern as you did on the figure. For instance, the width of chest is taken on the figure about midway of the depth of the armhole, as shown; so, place the tape about midway of the depth of the armhole on the pattern also. Do the same with the width of back and all the other measures. To insure accuracy in measuring the bust line, pin the back and front on a large piece of paper with the under-arm lines meeting near the armhole and the bust line appearing continuous. You can then readily measure the actual bust line. With the pattern sections in this position, measure the armscye, keeping the tape line standing up on its edge so as to be able to follow the curve readily and thus obtain an accurate measurement.

Next, pin the skirt sections, with hip lines touching, to a large section of paper. Complete the measures for the skirt just as you did for the waist, including the length measures, which, on both waist- and skirt-pattern sections, should be taken in the same position as they were on the figure.

45. Check Measures.—To save time, to insure accuracy, and to avoid confusion, it is advisable to make out a measure sheet containing the actual figures with which you will work in altering your pattern. These are called *check measures* and are always found to be a valuable help. In Table II is shown a form that may be used for this purpose. This may be copied on a separate sheet of paper for use or, if you prefer, your measurements may be entered in it for a permanent record. The first plan is the better, however, because of the changes in measures which very often take place and which make any sort of permanent record of little value.

46. In the first column, write your own measurements. In the second, write the measures with which you will work, for, in making the guide, you will use pattern pieces that represent only half of the figure. In the third column, mark the ease that is allowed in various parts of the pattern, remembering that, because you are working with half-pattern sections, only half of the allowance should be considered in the case of the bust, chest, back-width, and hip measures. The ease is generally as follows :

Back shoulder . .	½ inch longer than front
Bust line . . .	2 to 4 inches greater than bust measure
Chest line. .	¼ to ⅜ inch greater than chest measure
Back width . .	½ inch greater than width-of-back measure
Upper arm . .	1½ inches greater than upper-arm measure
Wrist . . .	½ to 1 inch greater than wrist measure
Hips . . .	1 to 2 inches greater than hip measure

For the measurements not listed, either the amount of ease is so variable, as in the armhole, that it is impossible to give a definite amount, or no ease is allowed, as in the length measures or the waist line.

TABLE II
CHECK MEASURES

	1	2	3	4	5	6
	Personal Measure	Working Measure	Amount of ease	Total 2+3	Pattern Measure	Amount of Alteration
Waist						
Bust . . .						
Neck . .						
Width of Chest .						
Width of Back .						
Shoulder Length .						
Front Length .						
Back Length .						
Armhole . . .						
Sleeve						
Upper Arm . .						
Inside Length .						
Wrist . . .						
Skirt						
Waist . . .						
Hip . . .						
Dart . . .						
Front Length .						
Side Length . .						
Back Length .						

In the fourth column, your working measure plus the amount of ease that is needed and always allowed, gives the actual measurements to which the guide pattern must be made to correspond. Column five is a list of the pattern measures taken on the pattern in approximately the same position as they would be taken on the figure. In the sixth column, the difference between your size and the pattern size is listed with a plus or minus sign in front of the figures to indicate whether the pattern should be enlarged or made smaller.

47. After you have taken and listed the measurements with the greatest care and accuracy, re-check them to be sure that they are as nearly perfect as you can make them. But, in following the table, remember that type, personality, and fashion all have a bearing on the ease wanted or desirable.

48. Final Decision Regarding Changes.—With your list of check measures completed, study it carefully in order to decide finally just what changes you will make. Keep in mind always that alterations are advisable only when a decided change is required in a pattern, for often the lines of a correctly proportioned pattern serve to conceal some slight defect in the figure that might be very evident if all the pattern measurements were made to correspond exactly with those of the individual. The length of the shoulder line, however, is an exception, for if this is but $\frac{1}{4}$ inch too long it will mark the difference between dowdiness and chic.

49. Method of Making Alterations.—When making a measurement smaller, it is merely necessary to lap the slashed edges the required amount and then pin them. Later, after you have checked the pattern to make sure of the accuracy of the alteration, the edges may be pasted. When enlarging, it is essential that an extra piece of paper be pinned under the spread edges, this also to be pasted in place later for a permanent effect.

Where a separation is made between two parts of a pattern, the gap in the outline of the pattern must be filled by drawing in new lines that will blend the two ends together. In certain cases, this will mean merely a straight line, but in others, particularly if the separation comes where the pattern outline is curved, such as in a sleeve cap, the new lines must be curved too. Strive always for a smooth, continuous effect

PLAIN-WAIST ALTERATIONS

50. After measurements of the figure and of the pattern have been accurately taken and recorded, you are ready to undertake the actual process of pattern alteration. Starting with the waist, because it is here that most adjustments are needed, the usual changes that are necessary are discussed and illustrated in this section. With an understanding of them, you should be able to adjust your pattern to make it right for your figure. Of course, there may be a certain amount of additional adjustment required in fitting, but, if the pattern changes are properly and accurately made, the altered pattern will make a n y pattern checked with it simpler to u s e because of the new ease in fitting.

51. A l t e r a - tion for Short- or Long - Waisted Figure —It fre- quently happens that figures are either long- or short - waisted, that is, that the waist line of a

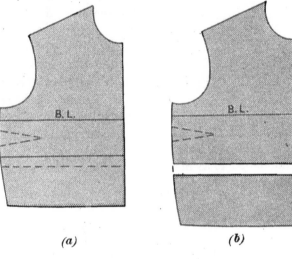

(a)　　　　　*(b)*

. Fig. 6

standard pattern is not in the correct position for them. To over- come this difficulty, slash across the entire width of the pattern, both back and front, midway between the bust and waist lines, as in Fig. 6, and then lap the edges the desired amount, as in view (*a*), or spread them as much as needed, as in view (*b*).

52. When the front or back alone needs shortening or lengthen- ing, the width of the alteration should graduate toward the side seam. For instance, a figure having a very full bust would require more length in front and no additional length in back. In such a case, make the separation as wide as necessary at the centre front and graduate its depth to nothing before you reach the under arm so as to leave this unchanged, as shown in Fig. 7. The same is true of a back that requires a change in length when the pattern is correct for the front, a condition that is encountered occasionally.

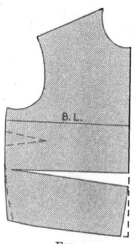

FIG. 7

In alterations of this type, the centre line slants away from the straight below the alteration, whether back or front. As illustrated, straighten the centre line, thus producing more width at the lower edge, which may be retained if the figure requires it, or taken off at the side seam if not, as shown by the dotted lines.

53. Alteration for Round Shoulders.—A round-shouldered person usually requires a pattern change that will provide the addition of length in the back, for such a figure generally has a greater centre-back length than the pattern measure. To obtain the needed length, slash the pattern at right angles to the centre back at the place where the figure seems to require it, generally about midway of the depth of the back armhole. Extend the slash to within a scant $\frac{1}{4}$ inch of the armhole edge, as in Fig. 8, view (a); and then separate the edges at the centre back the necessary amount. Straighten the back by drawing in a new centre-back line, as indicated. Then, from the under arm, remove the amount added here, unless the figure seems to require the extra fullness at the centre back.

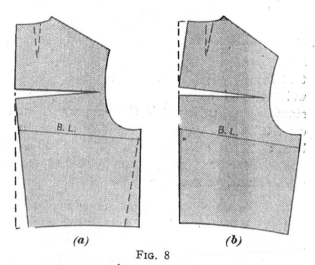

(a)   (b)

FIG. 8

54. If the back is round just below the neck line, as frequently is the case with the full, mature figure, keep the centre-back line below the slash on a straight line, and allow the fullness to come above, as shown in view (b). Take care of the extra width at the neck line by means of another dart, or use all the fullness at the neck line in dart-like tucks from the neck line down, the resulting fullness giving the necessary ease over the full part of the figure.

55. Alteration for Flat Chest.—When it is necessary to make a change in the back of a pattern to give the extra length needed by the round-shouldered figure, it frequently happens that the front-pattern section will require shortening because the figure having round shoulders is quite likely to have a flat chest too.

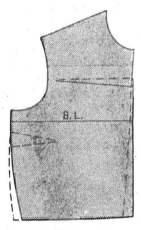

FIG. 9

To make such an alteration, slash the pattern at right angles to the centre front to within a scant $\frac{1}{4}$ inch of the armhole line, and then lap the slash at the centre front the desired amount, as shown at Fig. 9. The position of this slash should be regulated by the figure, but, as a rule, it should be about midway of the depth of the front armhole, corresponding to the position of the back slash. Straighten the centre-front line from the end of the crosswise slash, as shown, adding at the under arm the amount removed, if necessary.

56. Alteration for Large, Deep Armscye. Certain figures have a larger armscye measure than the average, generally due to muscular development, a variation

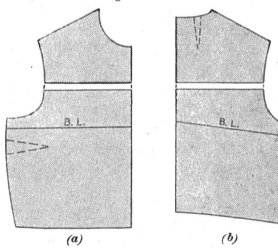

(a)   (b)

FIG. 10

that is not necessarily accompanied by a larger than average bust. For this, a length alteration should be made on both back and front, as shown in Fig. 10, views (a) and (b). Slash across the pattern pieces at about the half-way point of the armhole and straight to the centre front and centre back. Then separate the slashed edges the necessary amount, half in front and half in back; that is, if the armscye of the pattern is 1 inch too small, separate the front sections ½ inch and the back ½ inch, keeping the slash the same width entirely across the pattern piece.

Such an alteration will necessitate an enlargement in the armhole of the sleeve, as illustrated in Fig. 22, in order to have it fit into the new armhole. Also, the amount added to the armhole depth may need to be taken out below it in order to have the waist line in the proper position. In such a case, make the alteration similar to that shown in Fig. 6, view (a).

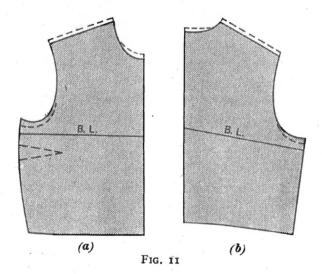

(a)   (b)

FIG. 11

57. Another alteration that enlarges the armscye, adds the extra size in two places, as shown in Fig. 11. To make this change for the front, add about one-fourth the necessary increase at the shoulder line, as shown in view (a), continuing the alteration evenly up to the neck line. Build up the front, as indicated, to prevent it from being too low. Next, enlarge the armscye at the under arm by marking a new curve, as shown, to add one-fourth the amount of the change needed. Repeat the alteration on the back, as shown in view (b).

58. Alteration for Small Armscye.—When the armscye is small, the pattern pieces may be slashed as directed in Art. 56 and lapped instead of being separated the desired amount. Or, changes may be made at the shoulder and under-arm, as shown in Fig. 12. For the front, mark off and trim away from the shoulders and neck one-fourth of the total amount to be decreased, and allow for another

one-fourth at the under arm by bringing it up to a shallower effect, as shown in view (*a*). Repeat the alteration on the back, as in view (*b*).

59. Alteration for Sway Back. The over - erect figure whose posture results in a hollow effect at the back - waist line with a definite outward curve below it, will generally find too much length in the back - waist pattern. To remove this length, slash the pattern

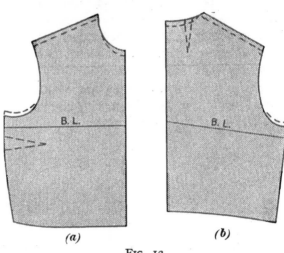

(a)   *(b)*

FIG. 12

at right angles to the centre back, about one-third of the under-arm length above the waist line because it is low on the figure that the alteration is required, slashing to within $\frac{1}{4}$ inch of the under-arm seam. Lap the slash at the centre back the desired amount, as shown in Fig. 13, tapering the depth of the lap to nothing near the under-arm seam. Straighten the centre-back line, as shown, adding the amount taken off here to the under-arm line if it is needed.

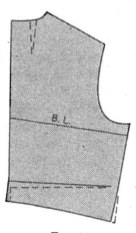

FIG. 13

60. Alteration for High Bust.—Another result of the over-erect posture is a longer-than-average front waist-length measure. The fact that the shoulders are thrown back generally causes a somewhat high chest and bust line, requiring an alteration that will overcome an effect of riding up in front. Because of the curves of the figure, the simple straight slash does not give quite as good results as the shaped one illustrated in Fig. 14.

To determine the placement of the slash, measure one-half the front bust line plus 1 inch from the centre front toward the under arm

and mark this point on the bust line, as at *a*, view (*a*). Now, from
1 to 2 inches below the bust line, slash straight in from the centre
front to a point just below *a*, and then slash upward diagonally
toward the half way point in the armhole, as shown, extending the
slash to within ¼ inch of the armhole edge. Separate the slash the
required amount at the centre front, as in view (*b*), and then redraw
the centre-front line, as shown. It will usually be found that the extra
fullness should be left in for the best effect, although it may be removed
at the under arm, as indicated. Also, the under-arm curve may be
trimmed out slightly, if necessary.

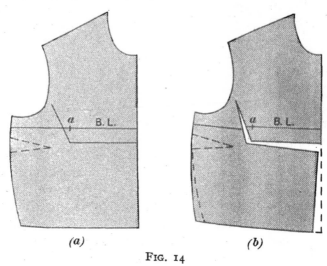

(*a*)   (*b*)

FIG. 14

61. Alteration for Large Bust.—When all measures of a pattern
except the bust line are correct and this must be increased, a simple
alteration in the front of the pattern will usually give proper results. To
increase width, slash the blouse pattern from the lower edge, having
the slash extend parallel with the centre front up to a point within
about ¼ inch of the middle of the shoulder line, as in Fig. 15, view (*a*).
Separate the slash the desired amount. This will give more fullness
at the lower edge of the blouse, but, as a rule, this will be found satisfactory.

62. When the bust measure is unusually large, especially in con-
junction with a large armhole measure, part of the amount can be
added to the pattern in the front, as shown in view (*a*), and the rest
at the under arm, back and front, as shown in view (*b*). For instance,
if 3 inches are to be added to the entire bust measure, or 1½ inches

to the pattern, separate the front slash ½ inch at the bust line, and add ½ inch to the under arm at the front and ½ inch at the back in the

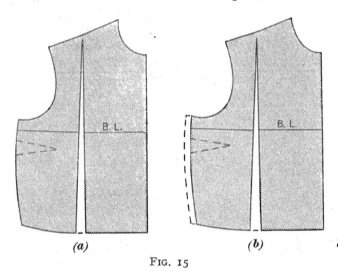

(a)   (b)

FIG. 15

same manner.   This plan will require a change in the sleeve, as illustrated in Fig. 23 (b) for it results in a larger armhole.

The under-arm alteration may be used alone without the front slash if the figure is such that the excess size seems to be located where this change will take care of it.

63. If the bust is full in front so that more length is required in the front blouse section, a deeper dart or an extra one of the same depth as the one provided in the pattern is usually supplied. To work out this plan satisfactorily, follow Fig. 16, first slashing the pattern and separating it as directed in Art. 61. Next, slash the pattern again from the under arm in to the first slash, having the direction of the second slash follow the upper line of the under-arm dart. Separate the cut edges of this slash an amount equal to the width of the original dart, at the most, or less if the figure does

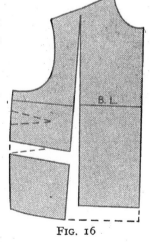

FIG. 16

not seem to require so much extra length. With the separation the same width throughout, pin the cut-out pattern piece in place, as shown. Then form a new lower-edge line and an elongated centre-front one until they meet. When basting in the darts, make both the same, that is, taper the lower one to nothing at its point, as shown, the extra material taking care of the larger bust size where needed. With the new dart basted, the length of the under arm remains unchanged.

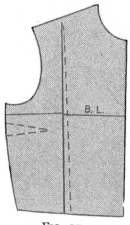

FIG. 17

64. Alteration for Small Bust.—To decrease the bust size, when a pattern larger than the bust measure has been provided to take care of broad shoulders, wide chest, and width of back, slash the pattern parallel with the centre front nearly up to the shoulder edge and then lap it, as shown in Fig. 17. This plan decreases the lower-edge width proportionately.

65. Alteration for Broad or Narrow Back.—When the back is broad, as it sometimes is in a figure of the athletic type, the pattern may be widened in a manner similar to the front, as shown in Fig. 15. If it is narrow, as when the figure is over-erect, the slash may be made and the edges lapped to take care of the necessary decrease in width, as for the front in Fig. 17.

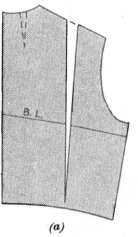

(a)

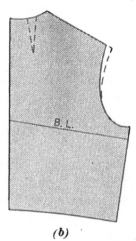

(b)

FIG. 18

66. Alteration for Broad or Narrow Shoulders.—The shoulder length of a garment has much to do with its appearance of correct fit as well as chic ; therefore, if the dress or blouse is to look well, this point must be correct. In many cases, when only a slight shortening is necessary, it can be taken care of during fitting. If it should be ½ inch or more, adjust the pattern.

67. If considerable width is to be added, slash the pattern down-ward parallel to the centre back from the centre of the shoulder line to within ¼ inch of the lower edge, as in Fig. 18, view (*a*), and separate the cut edges the desired amount, making the change on both back and front and keeping the back-shoulder line ½ inch longer than the front. The slight increase in the bust size will not usually be found objectionable. When the length is to be increased only a small amount, add it to the shoulder line at the armhole, both back and front, as in view (*b*).

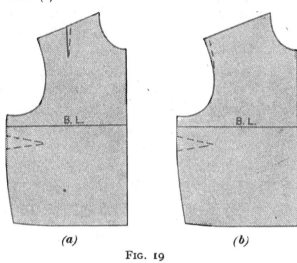

(a)   (b)

F<small>IG</small>. 19

68. To decrease shoulder length, form a dart-like fold in the shoulder length to take up the necessary amount, as shown in view (*a*), Fig. 19, pinning this in place, both back and front. For a slight alteration, trim away part of the length of the armhole, as indicated by the dotted line in view (*b*), making a similar change on the back.

69. Any change in shoulder length requires a change in the sleeve cap also, either for lengthening or for shortening. The process to follow is described in Art. 72 and illustrated in Fig. 21. Also, a sleeve change may be required when no pattern change was made in shoulder length. This will happen when a person having rather broad shoulders wants a short shoulder and finds the shoulder line of her original pattern satisfactory even though it is short by actual measurement. In such a case, length must be added to the sleeve cap, as in Fig. 21, view (*a*), in order to have it fit up over the shoulder curve without drawing.

PLAIN-SLEEVE ALTERATIONS

70. A sleeve, to be correct, must fit into the armscye properly, it must fit well for the entire length of the arm, and its elbow point and wrist must be truly located. When there is a variation from the average in figure, one or more of these features require adjustment. The necessary changes should be made in the pattern before cutting in order to save the time and effort of fitting and alteration in the garment fabric.

71. Alteration for Long or Short Arm.—Because a sleeve is so designed that the elbow point is intended to correspond with the

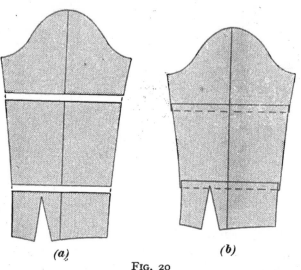

elbow when the sleeve is worn, it is not correct to lengthen or shorten the sleeve at the wrist. For correct results, follow Fig. 20, view (*a*), if you wish to lengthen the sleeve, slashing through the width both above and below the elbow, as in-dicated. Sepa-

(a)   *(b)*

FIG. 20

rate the cut edges the desired amount and blend the edges. For arms that need additional length in only one place, make a single alteration, either above or below the elbow.

To shorten the sleeve, slash in the same way but lap the cut edges the necessary amount, as in view (*b*), both above and below the elbow if shortening is needed in both places, or in either one of these posi-tions, depending on the arm length.

72. Alteration in Length of Sleeve Cap.—If the shoulder line has been lengthened or shortened, or if the size of the armhole has been changed for any reason, a corresponding change must be made in the sleeve. To make a slight alteration in the length of the sleeve cap, when the shoulder seam has been shortened, follow Fig. 21, view (a), adding an amount to the sleeve that corresponds to the amount

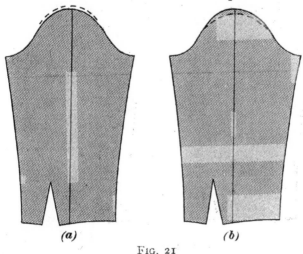

(a)   *(b)*

Fig. 21

removed from the shoulder length. Taper the depth of the altera-tion to nothing along the sides of the cap, as illustrated.

To decrease the length of the sleeve cap, mark with a dotted line and trim away the necessary amount at the tip, as shown in view (b), graduating to nothing at each side the amount removed.

73. When the length of the armhole has been made greater, as in Fig. 10, slash the sleeve pattern crosswise in a position that will correspond approximately to the posi-tion of the slashes in the waist back and front, and separate the slashed edges the required amount, as in Fig. 22. Notice that the line that blends the cut edges curves outward a trifle in order to give the slight extra ease to the cap.

Fig. 22

74. Alteration for Large Arm.—To in-crease the width of the sleeve, slash it through its lengthwise centre from the top almost to the lower edge on the centre line and separate the cut edges the desired amount, as in Fig. 23, view (a). Or, as shown in view (b), increase the sleeve size by adding one-half the needed amount on each side of the under arm.

Careful observation of the arm that the sleeve is intended to fit will help you to decide which alteration to use. The arm that is full

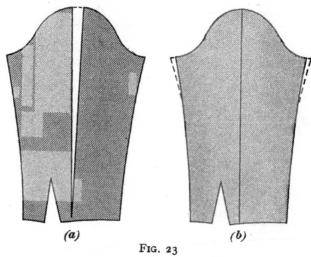

(a)   *(b)*

FIG. 23

on top will find the slashing alteration better, while excess size concentrated at the under part of the arm will need the other kind of change. The under-arm alteration is always used when the bust size has been increased by adding to the under arm, back and front, as shown in Fig. 15 (*b*). For the very large upper arm, these two alterations may be combined, some of the needed extra width added at the

FIG. 24

slash and the remainder at the under arm. In either case, the alterations will generally taper to the wrist, although, if extra width is needed for the entire length of the sleeve, the alteration may be the same depth throughout.

When sleeve fullness is in fashion, the extra width may be gathered or pleated into the armhole, but if the sleeve is to fit smoothly into the armhole seam, the size of the armhole must be changed to accommodate the enlarged sleeve. The proper alterations to make are described in Arts. 56 and 57 and illustrated in Figs. 10 and 11.

75. It is sometimes necessary to combine alterations for a large upper arm and a short sleeve cap, particularly for the small-boned but excessively fat figure whose upper arm has an out-of-proportion girth measure and seems to curve outward between the shoulder and

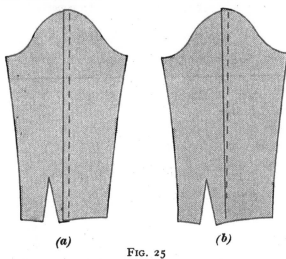

(a)   *(b)*

FIG. 25

elbow. To make such changes, follow Fig. 24, slashing the sleeve through the lengthwise centre to about the elbow point, and then crosswise at the end of the first slash, as shown. The second slash may extend to within ¼ inch of the edges on each side or considerably less, depending on the amount of spread necessary at the top. Separate the edges at the top, which will lengthen the cap at the same time. Such a change requires an enlargement of the armhole of the garment, additional length added at the shoulder seam, and a small amount trimmed out underneath, as in Fig. 11, giving the best results.

76. Alteration for Small Arm.—To decrease the width of the sleeve, slash and lap the edges, as in Fig. 25, extending the slash for the same depth throughout, as at view *(a)*, or tapering it to nothing as it approaches the wrist, as in view *(b)*.

FIG. 26

77. When only a small amount needs to be removed from the sleeve width, trim off the under-arm edges on each side, as shown in Fig. 26. This alteration may be combined with that shown in Fig. 25, view *(b)*.

78. When the sleeve is decreased in size, an alteration to decrease the armhole size of the garment is also necessary. · Therefore, follow Fig. 12 and Art. 58 so that the sleeve may fit properly into position.

PLAIN-SKIRT ALTERATIONS

79. Changes in a skirt pattern are simple and easy to accomplish, but the merit and helpfulness of a carefully fitted skirt pattern must not be overlooked. Indeed, one that has been correctly adjusted to the figure will prove to be just as helpful to you as your waist and your sleeve patterns, particularly if there is any variation from the average, as there often is, especially in the hip size.

80. Altering Skirt Length.—Because of the proportion on which a skirt pattern is built, it is not wise to shorten or lengthen merely at the lower edge. Instead, for a moderate-size alteration, make one slash, as shown in Fig. 27, midway between the hip line and the lower edge, spreading the edges the desired amount to lengthen, as shown in view (a), and lapping them to shorten, as in view (b).

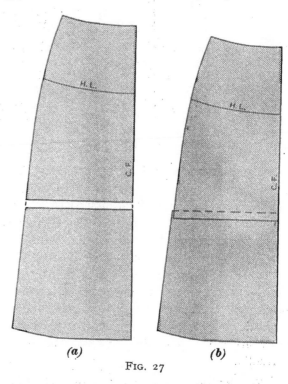

(a)   *(b)*

Fig. 27

If a generous amount is to be added or taken away, make two slashes, one at one-third of the distance from the hip line to the lower edge below the hip line, and the other this same distance above the lower edge. Spread or lap as usual, making half of the alteration at each slash.

81. Alteration for Prominent Abdomen.—The figure having a prominent abdomen will have a front length greater than the average and out of proportion to her side- and back-skirt lengths. To adjust the pattern for such a variation, follow Fig. 28, slashing the front-pattern section between the waist and hip lines where the figure seems to require it, from the centre front to within ¼ inch of the side seam, as shown. Spread the desired amount, then mark in a new centre line. If the extra fullness is not desirable, although it generally is, it may be trimmed away at the side seam, as shown by the dotted line, or taken up in darts each side of the centre front.

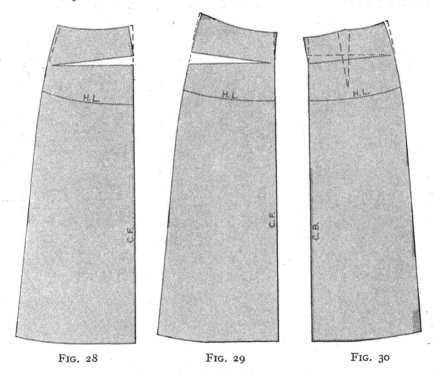

FIG. 28   FIG. 29   FIG. 30

82. Alteration for Prominent Hips.—Certain figure types have a longer than average side length caused by hips that are prominent at the side. To alter a pattern for such a figure, follow Fig. 29, slashing the front pattern from the side seam to within ¼ inch of the centre front and midway between the waist and hip lines. Separate the slashed edges the required amount, as shown. Then straighten the centre-line, and add a corresponding amount at the side seam so that the size of the waist line will remain correct. Repeat this alteration on the back pattern piece so that back and front side seams will be exactly the same length.

83. Alteration for Sway-Back Figure.—To make a pattern suitable for a shorter-than-average length from the waist line to the hip line in back, slash the back-pattern piece between the waist and hip lines, as in Fig. 30, extending the slash to within ¼ inch of the side seam, and lap it the necessary amount. If necessary, re-draw the centre-back line and the side seam line.

84. Altering Skirt Width.—When there is a slight change to be made in skirt width, small amounts, that is, up to ½ inch, can be added

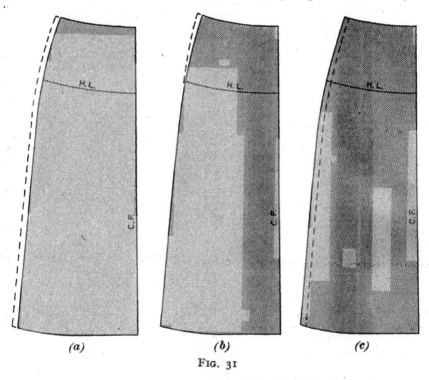

(a)   (b)   (c)

FIG. 31

or taken away at each of the side seams. Follow Fig. 31, view (a), when width is to be added, having the alteration the same width throughout.

When only the waist line is large, the amount may be graduated from the waist line to the hip line, as shown in view (b). In this case, as much as 1 inch may be added to the waist line at each side seam.

85.. Width may be decreased by trimming away a small amount of the skirt width, as indicated in view (c). This alteration may also be graduated if merely the waist line is to be reduced, the necessary amount taken away at the waist line, and the alteration tapered down to nothing at the hip.

86. Altering Lower Skirt Width.—To enlarge a skirt at the hip line without disturbing the waist line, mark the half-way point on the waist line and slash from the lower edge to within $\frac{1}{4}$ inch of this point, parallel to the centre front, and separate the slashed edges, as shown in Fig. 32, view (*a*). To make a skirt smaller, lap the slashed edges, as in view (*b*). In both cases, adjust the lower - edge width if you wish, trimming a w a y the excess flare at the side seam when extra width is added, as in view (*a*), and providing the regulation amount of flare when width has been taken away, as in view (*b*).

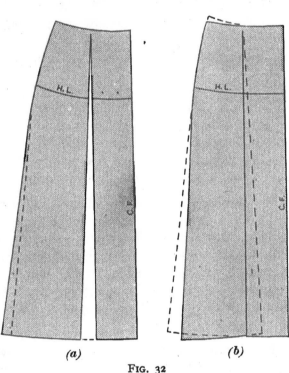

(*a*)   (*b*)

FIG. 32

87. These alterations, while shown on only the front-pattern pieces, should be applied to the back similarly. However, the proportions of the figure must always be observed carefully first, for there are certain types who will require the alteration only in front or only in back. So that it will not coincide with the dart, locate the back slash about 1 inch from the dart edge at the waist line and parallel to and towards the centre back. If the size of the waist line is to be increased, the slash may be continued for the entire length of the pattern and the slash spread the same amount throughout.

TESTING THE ALTERED PATTERN

PREPARATION

88. After all needed changes have been made in your pattern and it has been checked for accuracy, the correctness of its fit must be tested before it can be used to check other patterns with absolute certainty as to the results. So, with the aid of your altered pattern, a muslin model should be made and fitted to the figure with precision. This plan will make it possible to take care of, in fitting, those small variations from the average that are not so much a matter of measurement as of posture and figure development, and therefore entirely individual.

Then, after the garment has been fitted and accurately marked, it should be ripped apart and any changes transferred to your heavy paper pattern. However, one guide pattern should not be considered in too permanent a manner, for both the figure and the silhouette change, and consequently a new pattern should be made at least once a year, and probably oftener, depending on circumstances.

89. Material Requirements.—To get the best results from fitting, the fabric used for the model should be firm without being stiff, such as unbleached muslin that is pliable and evenly woven but not heavy. For those who prefer it, a soft gingham having a woven check is also suggested, because the grain of the material can readily be kept straight in such fabric. Of any 35-inch fabric, the average figure will require about $3\frac{1}{2}$ yards for a complete guide pattern of waist, skirt, and sleeve.

90. Cutting the Model.—In a general way, the cutting guide included with the tissue-paper or commercial pattern you have used as a foundation, is the best aid you can follow in placing the various parts of your pattern on the material. Place the centre front and centre back of the waist and skirt on lengthwise folds, the centre line of the sleeve on a straight lengthwise thread, and the sleeve on a double thickness so that two sleeves will be cut. Cut with at least $\frac{5}{8}$ inch seams and a 3-inch hem. Mark all construction aids, clip the notches, mark-stitch the position of the darts in blouse and skirt, indicate the centre-front and centre-back lines with basting-stitches that will contrast in colour with the muslin, and then remove the pattern from the fabric.

91. Basting the Model.—Clip the mark-stitches first, then pin in and baste the darts. Baste the shoulder and the sleeve seams, including the sleeve dart, leaving the sleeve open for 2 or 3 inches so that the hand can slip through readily. If your pattern is of the type that has some fullness in the waist, run in gathering-threads along the lower edge, back and front, to take care of it, and adjust evenly. Then join the skirt and waist sections with overlapped seams, centre-front and centre-back lines as well as notches matching.

Pin, then baste the under-arm seams except for a 6- to 8-inch space at the left waist line for ease in putting the garment on and taking it off, keeping the waist-line seams in line on both sides.

Pin the sleeve and under-arm seams together, as at *a*, Fig. 33, also the corresponding notches of sleeve and armhole, as at *b* and *c*. Next, pin the top of the sleeve to the shoulder line, as at *d*, also at *e* and *f*, about $1\frac{1}{4}$ inches on each side of the shoulder seam, keeping the sleeve smooth between these pins. Then, with the hand in the position shown, holding the edges of sleeve and armhole, roll these back over the fingers as indicated, when the sleeve will take approximately the same position that it will have when worn, with no apparent fullness.

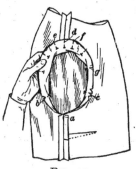

FIG. 33

Half-way between point *f* and the notch *c*, place another pin, as at *g*, dividing any fullness equally, as shown. Place as many pins around the armhole as are necessary, always dividing the ease evenly. Then baste in the sleeve with small stitches. Finally, slash the centre-front for about 6 inches so that the garment will slip over the head readily.

FITTING

92. Slip the model on, adjust it at the waist line, centre-front and centre-back lines in correct position, and pin up the under-arm and the wrist openings and the centre-front slash, taking up as little material as possible at this point. Place a straight strip of material as a belt around the waist line, pinning this in the correct position.

You may find that the basted model will require no alterations. In such an event, it may be removed with the assurance that the altered pattern from which it was cut will prove to be a very satisfactory guide to be used as directed later. Make sure, however, by careful measurement, that the skirt length is even and accurate.

Keep in mind, as you proceed with the fitting, that a model intended for a guide pattern should fit in an easy manner, but apparently without any fullness or surplus width through the shoulders, neck, and armholes.   Before making any changes, study the model carefully to determine just what the cause of any ill-fitting details may be and how you can best remedy the difficulty.   Then, in making any changes that may be required in the seam lines, aim to keep them in their correct position on the figure.   The following suggestions are

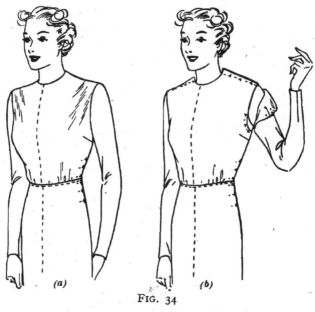

FIG. 34

applicable to the fitting of an actual garment as well as a guide pattern.

93. Altering for Square Shoulders.—The figure having high shoulders will cause the garment to wrinkle from the tip of the shoulder towards the centre front, as shown in Fig. 34, view (a). To overcome this feature, rip the sleeve out at the shoulder seam, and the shoulder seam itself, and then repin the shoulder seam, making it as shallow as needed at the shoulder tip and deepening it as it approaches the neck line, as shown in view (b).   For some figures, you may find it necessary to make this alteration deeper on the back or on the front, while in others, an even change is best.

The result of such a change is a deeper armscye curve at the under arm, which will require building up if the sleeve is to fit properly again. Therefore, pin small sections of muslin in both back and front as shown, trimming these in order to give an effect as similar as possible to the original armscye curve. Replace the sleeve by pinning.

94. Altering for Sloping Shoulders.—When the shoulders slope, the wrinkles in the waist are likely to extend from neck line to under arm, as shown in Fig. 35, view (a). To take care of this figure variation, rip the shoulder seam and repin it, deepening it toward the

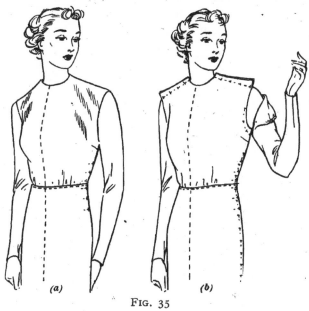

(a)   (b)

FIG. 35

armhole, as shown in view (b). This change will draw up the underarm curve and make the armscye smaller, necessitating a trimming out of the curve. Mark the new line with pins, as shown. Then, after removing the garment, rebaste the sleeves in place along the new line, assure yourself by a second fitting that the line is correct, and finally trim out the armhole.

95. Altering for Loose Back-Neck Line.—As shown in Fig. 36, view (a), the back-neck line of the garment may stand away from the figure and also appear somewhat low in cut. To tighten the neck line, deepen the darts, if they are included in your pattern, and, if not, pin in small darts until the neck line of the garment lies close to the figure, as shown in view (b). If the curve seems somewhat low, build it up by inserting a section of muslin of the proper size, as shown, and trimming off its upper edge for a graceful neck-line curve.

96. Altering for Tight Back-Neck Line.—Another fitting problem that may be met on a figure with over-erect posture is that of the tight back-neck line, as shown in Fig. 37, view (*a*). To overcome this, trim out the neck seam to a deeper curve, first marking the curve with pins, as in view (*b*).

97. Altering the Side-Seam Line.—It may be found that an alteration is required at the under-arm seam, because the garment seems a little too small or large, or because the position of the seam is not straight when viewed from the direct side.

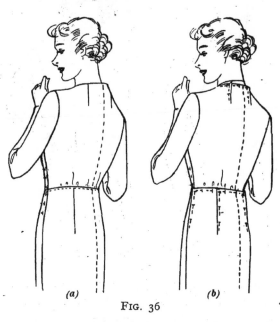

(a)   (b)

FIG. 36

When the garment seems large, pin in the seam as shown in Fig. 35, view (*b*), starting at the waist line, continuing up toward the arm-hole, where the alteration should graduate to nothing, and downwards to a point somewhat below the hip line. If the garment is small, follow a reverse process, that is, let out the seam as much as is necessary. Make the alteration the same on both sides, at all times keeping the centre-front and centre-back lines in correct position.

98. It may happen also that the garment fits well but that the direction of the side seam below the waist line is not good. If it slants to the front, improve its position by first ripping the seam and then repinning it, making the back seam deeper and the front seam more shallow. If the seam slants to the back, make the front seam deeper and the back one less than the regulation ⅜ inch.

99. An even side seam alteration may extend only from the waist line down. Certain figures, such as the type very slender above the waist and the one full above the waist with waist and hip small in proportion, will find some extra ease in the waist portion more becoming, as shown in Fig. 37, view (b). In such an event, the extra material may be eased in with the regulation waist-line fullness.

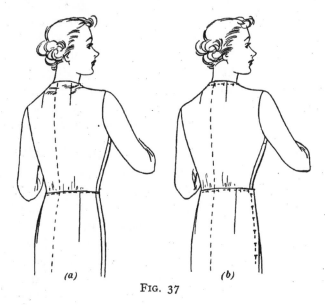

FIG. 37

100. Altering the Waist Line.—When the waist line is too large for the figure, changes should be made at the side seams as well as in the back waist-line darts, as indicated in Fig. 36, view (b). Deepen the darts by taking up just a small amount on each, and deepen the side seams as shown. If the waist line is tight, follow a reverse process, letting out both darts and side seams.

101. Altering the Wrist Size.—As a general rule, the only alteration needed at the wrist is one that will make the sleeve smaller at this point. When, therefore, the sleeve seems large, as in Fig. 38, view (a), deepen the dart as much as is necessary for a snug fit, as shown in view (b). If the alteration seems too great to be taken care of in one place, take out some of the ease in the dart and the remainder in the sleeve seam.

102. Hanging the Skirt.—When all necessary changes have been made, mark the skirt length. Determine on a fashionable and becoming position for the hem turn, mark, in the preferred manner the line decided on, and turn the lower edge up on the marked line. Examine carefully and adjust where necessary.

103. Deciding on Alterations.—In putting into practice any of the suggestions given on fitting, remember that you must make your own decision as to just what changes are needed, considering always, as has been stated previously, that the original good lines of the pattern must be retained at all costs. Before making any changes, it is well, therefore, to ask yourself the question, " Will I improve the effect ? " Also, it must be understood that perhaps only one of the fitting changes illustrated will need to be made, although if several will make an improvement in the guide pattern, use as many as you deem necessary for a satisfactory muslin model.

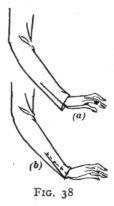

(a)

(b)

Fig. 38

COMPLETING THE PATTERN

104. Steps after Fitting.—When you have satisfied yourself that the garment is perfectly suited to the figure, that all seam lines are correct, and that all joinings are in proper position, remove the model and mark with pencil or tailor's chalk all alterations that you have made. Also, mark the outlines of all darts. Next, rip the garment apart, including the darts, and true up all seam allowances to $\frac{3}{8}$ inch on all edges, measuring accurately. Trim off the hem allowance to $2\frac{1}{2}$ inches, a width that is considered average for most materials. Press all parts of the muslin, being very careful not to stretch any curved edges, such as the neck line or the armscye of sleeve or waist.

105. Cutting the Permanent Pattern.—Provide yourself with lengths of heavy paper of a quality that is pliable but strong, a very heavy smooth-finished wrapping paper usually giving the best results. Such paper can generally be purchased in stationers. Because your muslin guide is to be used for cutting the permanent pattern, fold the front and back waist and skirt sections on the centre lines, and pin carefully along the fold and entirely around the cut edges, which should, of course, meet evenly. Now place the muslin pattern on a single thickness of your paper, pin it securely, and cut neatly, thus providing half a waist front and back, half a skirt front and back, and one sleeve.

Mark all notches accurately ; then, with your tracing wheel, mark the dart lines through to the paper underneath. Remove the muslin pattern. Then mark the bust, hip, and centre sleeve lines on your paper pattern. You now have a plain guide, or foundation, pattern that fits your figure properly and that may be used to check up any other patterns that you desire to use from time to time.

USING YOUR GUIDE PATTERN

106. An example of the type of checking that can be done with your guide pattern is shown in Figs. 39, 40, and 41. In Fig. 39 is illustrated a dress design consisting of a separate waist and skirt joined at the waist line, with full-length panel effects, front and back, further distinguished by effectively placed shirring. In Figs. 40 and 41, the method of checking the cutting guide for this particular design is indicated.

FIG. 39

You will note that the various sections have been pinned together so as to approximate as nearly as possible the finished effect of front- and back-waist sections, skirt sections, and sleeve. These pinned-up pattern parts are matched to the corresponding sections of the guide pattern, carefully compared, and then, where necessary, are altered in order to have the lines of the pattern being tested follow those of the guide pattern. This procedure will insure a finished garment that will fit with the same precision as did your guide pattern, because its outlines are the same even though it contains various fashion features not found in the guide.

107. Procedure in Checking.—As the first step in the checking process, pin together the various parts that go to make up each section. Of course, in some cases, where the garment to be made is simple, this may not be required, for if the blouse front, for instance, is all in one piece, there is nothing required except the actual testing. However, where there are allowances for front hems, tucks, pleats, shirrings, and so on, these should all be pinned in so as to give the pattern the appearance that one-half of the garment cut from it would have when completed.

When the pattern pieces have been prepared, place each one over the corresponding guide pattern sections, centre lines matching, and have the shoulder lines of the front- and back-waist sections as well as the waist lines of the skirt, match, if possible. If the shoulder and waist lines of the pattern to be tested and the guide pattern do not match, have them come as close together as possible, while keeping the centre lines exactly together. Pin the pattern pieces to your guide pattern.

Notice in Figs. 40 and 41 the differences that are apparent, and the changes that will need to be made in order to have the new design a

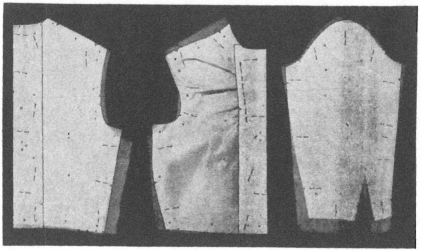

Fɪɢ. 40

satisfactory fit. Where necessary, therefore, build out the new tissue-paper pattern or trim off excess width so as to have its outlines follow those of your foundation pattern as closely as possible.

108. Important Points to Consider.—For the best results, you must be constantly alert for certain matters that you are likely to meet in this work and take care of them when the need arises. For instance, fashion always plays an important part in the design of a pattern. In the case illustrated, notice that the blouse back of the new pattern is definitely narrower at the under-arm seam than is the guide pattern, and that the under-arm line is higher. This is due to the somewhat close-fitting effect that the fashion of the season requires the finished garment to have. So, it is important to use your judg-ment in determining whether or not an alteration should be made.

If the foundation pattern has been fitted to your figure in a way that pleases you, by all means make the alteration. But, if some of the smartness of a particular design would be lost by an appearance of ease instead of trim smoothness, it is, perhaps, best to follow the under-arm lines of the new pattern. This would mean that the under

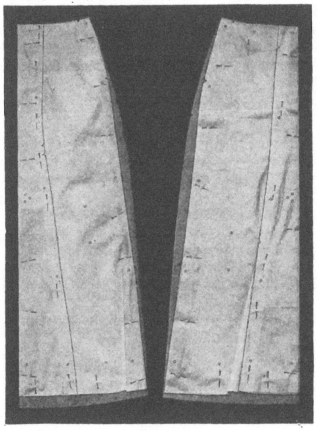

FIG. 41

arm of the sleeve should remain unchanged too, the shape of the cap alone being altered in this case.

Darts are another feature that must be considered. Ordinarily they should be left unpinned in the pattern being tested, especially if they are located in the same positions as in your foundation pattern. But, often, darts are absorbed in some trimming feature. Notice that the pattern being tested shows no dart in the front-waist section. This is due to the fact that the panel front and the side fullness have the same effect on the grain of the material that a shoulder dart would have. Because of this, the darts of your guide pattern, under-arm, shoulder, or both, must be pinned in during the testing.

The same is true of the back-skirt section, which takes up the usual back dart in the joining of the back panel to the side skirt section, meaning that the back-skirt dart should be pinned in before the skirt pattern is tested.

Notice also that, contrary to rule, the front-shoulder line is longer than the back. This is due to a design feature, the space between the shoulder notches in front being eased into the corresponding space in back.

EXAMINATION QUESTIONS

(1) What do you consider the main point of difference between commercial and drafted patterns ?

(2) Describe the uses of perforations and markings on commercial patterns.

(3) Why is it important to select the proper size in a pattern ?

(4) (a) How should a person stand when measurements are being taken ? (b) Describe the placing of the guide tape at the waist line.

(5) (a) Give three reasons for removing seam allowances of the guide pattern. (b) Describe the position and method of drawing in the foundation lines.

(6) Describe the method of measuring : (a) the bust line ; (b) the armscye curve of your pattern.

(7) Describe two alterations for making the armscye of a pattern smaller.

(8) Why should length alterations in sleeves generally be made in two places ?

(9) Describe both the waist (bodice) and the skirt alterations required for a sway-back figure.

(10) What change is needed in fitting when the shoulders are : (a) square ? (b) sloping ?

(11) How should a tissue-paper pattern be prepared in order to check it with the guide pattern ?